M000281452

VIEW FROM THE COCKPIT

VIEW FROM THE COCKPIT

DAVID BROWN

Airlife
England

Acknowledgements

I would like to thank the following individuals who have given permission for extracts of my articles to be reprinted. These include: Wayman Dunlap of *Pacific Flyer*, Barry Wheeler of *Air International*, Peter Howard of *Jane's Defence Weekly*, Allan Burney of *Aircraft Illustrated*, and Ed Schnepf of Challenge Publications.

First published in the UK in 1995
by Airlife Publishing Ltd

British Library Cataloguing in Publication Data
A catalogue record for this book
is available from the British Library

ISBN 1 85310 302 0

Typeset by Servis Filmsetting Ltd, Manchester
Printed by St Edmundsbury Press, Bury St Edmunds, Suffolk

Airlife Publishing Ltd.
101 Longden Road, Shrewsbury SY3 9EB

Contents

1
The Ultimate High

The staccato bark of the engine is loud in my ears as I turn the tiny red, white and blue biplane on to the runway. Making small corrections on the brake pedals I align the nose carefully along the grey strip of runway, then touch the brakes. The biplane shudders to a halt and my eyes flicker across the gauges to check that oil pressure and temperature are within limits. All is in order and the runway is clear.

Now there is nothing left but to take a deep breath . . . and go. My left hand firmly pushes the throttle lever forward. As the noise of the engine swells to a shattering explosion of power the acceleration pushes me firmly back into my seat. At this instant I always have a momentary feeling of kinship with the human cannonball seen at the circus years ago, and I wonder at his thoughts at the moment of launch . . . perhaps a fervent wish that he had chosen an alternate way of life. But for him – and for myself – there is no going back. For this is the cockpit of a Pitts Special, one of the best competition aerobatic airplanes in the world today.

Despite the pressure of my right foot on the rudder pedal the Pitts tries to slide towards the left-hand side of the narrow runway, pulled by the engine torque of the two hundred horsepower Lycoming. But then the rudder starts to bite on the air and the biplane runs straight. Another instant and as flying speed is reached the Pitts rockets skywards. The field drops away below. With the take-off now accomplished I have a brief chance to relax and enjoy the view. During the climb I look out and marvel once more at this chariot in which I ride the sky. The lower wings extend barely eight feet to either side. Painted a brilliant white, each has a red and blue sunburst sweeping back from the leading edge. It is a no-nonsense, aggressive paint scheme for an aircraft designed without compromise for its unique role, and it suits this machine perfectly.

I twist in my seat to look for other aircraft, admiring the beauty of the surrounding mountains and the patterns of the citrus groves in the Santa Clara valley below. I am alone in the sky and from this lofty perch I have a spectacular view. Beyond the rugged mountains which ring the valley I can see south as far as the coast. On the horizon the Channel Islands float on an impossibly blue Pacific.

It is Saturday afternoon and I am far away from the world of designing supersonic aircraft which occupies my working life; a world of computers and arcane mathematical formulae. This is flying reduced to its bare essentials. It is a spartan cockpit. As the Pitts climbs I shiver as the wind searches out the chinks around the perspex canopy. Under my right hand the control stick trembles imperceptibly as the ailerons sense the airflow rushing over the wing.

It is a perfect day in this cloudless sky and I find myself humming tunelessly, the sound inaudible above the roar of the engine. In sheer exuberance I slam the stick over to the right. The smoggy blur of Los Angeles, lying on the horizon off my right shoulder, disappears and the world rotates. I centralize the stick and Los Angeles reappears inverted on my left. The peaks of the surrounding mountains now jut down towards me like stalactites, while beneath the lower wings a limitless expanse of blue sky stretches from horizon to horizon. Despite the incongruity of this scene I am still sitting comfortably in my seat, restrained by my harness, while the fuel-injected Lycoming continues to roar reassuringly in my ears.

I twitch the stick and the Pitts rolls back to level flight. Peering through a cat's cradle of bracing wires I check again that no other aircraft are in my vicinity. Satisfied that I am still alone in this part of the heavens, I prepare for the self-imposed task which lies ahead. Today I will be attempting to perfect a sequence of aerobatic manoeuvres written in pictorial shorthand on a card taped to the instrument panel.

This is the part of flying I enjoy the most. Aerobatics is challenging and to me introduces a sense of adventure in our over-regulated civilisation. Speed is not the challenge; it is the extension of my personal limits which is the challenge, together with the precise control of this diminutive biplane through an intricate series of manoeuvres.

I ease the stick sideways and the world below tilts as I turn. My eyes search for a thin ribbon of grey which tracks across the green and brown patchwork of the fields. This is Highway 126 connecting the cities of Santa Paula and Fillmore. Today this road will serve as my reference line, and two convenient road junctions just over half a mile apart will serve as my airspace limits. In competition I would fly within the limits of a box of similar length and width which would be marked on the ground. The top of the box is at three thousand five hundred feet. I would lose marks by trespassing over any of the edges.

There is a strange paradox in aerobatics. I have the ultimate freedom, such as no bird has ever known, of moving freely in three dimensions, careless of the position of the earth. But at the same time my flight through space is ruled by the tightest discipline. The g-forces imposed by the rapid changes of direction are punishing both to man and machine. My apparent weight will vary until I weigh momentarily up to five times my normal weight; the next moment I can be weightless. I must perform my manoeuvres only

8

within a narrow range of speeds. If I am too slow the wings will stall and the Pitts will quit flying; too fast and I could overstress the aircraft or risk blacking out as the blood is forced away from my head by the g-force. I must constantly be aware of my altitude. The ground is very unforgiving of mistakes.

The altimeter needle stops at precisely three thousand five hundred feet and I turn until the biplane is flying parallel to the road. I pull the throttle back and the engine's roar fades. As speed decays the controls become sloppy and the stall-warning horn blows a strident note. I kick the right rudder pedal and the Pitts yaws to the right, tucks its nose down and begins to spin. Sunlight and shadow chase across the instrument panel. Over the nose I see the valley floor rotating. Once round and the road reappears. Now the rotation is really winding up. Two turns are completed before I push hard on the left pedal, come forward with the stick and the little biplane obediently snaps out of the spin.

Nose down, the Pitts accelerates and I sneak a glance at the card on the panel. My next manoeuvre is a Cuban eight. This involves performing the first part of a loop and continuing through into an inverted dive before I roll right side up again. By joining two such manoeuvres together I will draw a huge figure eight lying on its side in the sky.

The noise of the wind rises to a scream as the Pitts accelerates in the dive. At one hundred and sixty miles per hour I pull back on the stick, Gravity pushes me firmly down into the seat and the biplane rockets skywards. I glance out at the left wingtip to check that the wings are level and as the Pitts goes over onto its back and begins to slow I look up, over the top wing, to search for the road, easing forward on the stick at the same time. The biplane is now floating across the top of the loop on an almost ballistic trajectory. My eyes find the road and I correct with stick and rudder as the engine torque tries to pull the nose sideways and the nose drops into the inverted dive. Gravity is now forcing me against the straps, trying to pull me out of the cockpit and into the void below. I ignore these unusual sensations, concentrating on the dial of the airspeed indicator and the position of the nose as it tracks along the road.

Then it all goes wrong.

As I push the stick over and roll out of the inverted dive the road slides ten degrees off to one side of the nose and I am now angling away across the valley. I am annoyed with myself, my frustration made worse because I know what is wrong. During the roll-out I neglected to push the stick far enough forward. This inevitably caused the nose to drift off to the right during the roll. It's lucky that today no judges are watching. In competition I would lose points for an error like that. But I have to be honest in judging myself. Quick work with stick and rudder gets me back on line and the wires begin to wail again as I accelerate once more in the dive for the second half of the Cuban eight. Back on the stick and the Pitts arcs upwards into the sun and floats across the top of the circle. Now heading downhill I must wait until the wail of the wind swells again, judging the moment to roll upright again so that this part of the manoeuvre is symmetrical with the first.

Remember now to keep that stick forward and . . . now . . . slam the stick over to the left until it hits my knee. The world rotates smartly through 180 degrees and as I centralise the stick the nose is tracking down the road.

Progress at last.

Next comes a hammerhead stall. I pull into level flight, check my speed, and pull back hard on the stick until the Pitts is climbing vertically, slowing as gravity overcomes its momentum. Timing is critical now. If I'm too late on the rudder the Pitts will come to a stop in mid-air, then slide ignominiously tail-first towards the ground. As the wailing of the wind dies away I push hard on the left rudder pedal. The Pitts cartwheels to the left and the nose knifes past the horizon and down across the fields until it is pointing straight down towards the ground. The pattern of the orange groves below expands rapidly towards me and I pull back on the stick to regain level flight, where I check the speed and then roll inverted.

I'm working hard. In this inverted position my arms and legs are heavy and I am sweating despite the cold air on this winter day. Keeping the stick forward I push it slowly over to the left, with a touch of rudder to co-ordinate the half roll back to level flight. As the wings come level I see that the nose is still pointing along the road. I'm pleased with that.

Rolling into a turn to reverse my direction, I glance over the side to check my position, then do a double-take in disbelief. I'm a hundred yards past the junction on the highway marking the limit of my imaginary box of airspace. A moment of despair. How could I have made such an error? But already I can see the cause on the ground. Half a mile below me a tractor is towing a drifting tail of dust through the orange groves. There is a strong wind now blowing down the valley, although it was calm when I took off. The wind has blown me out of the box.

There is no time to brood over my mistake. The next manoeuvre must be completed speedily if I am not to compound my error by flying out of the other end of the box. I pull back the throttle, get the speed down to 100 mph, then push the right pedal hard, simultaneously bringing the stick back and over to the right. The Pitts shudders, then whips round in a snap roll so violent that I must immediately reverse the controls to kill the rotation. In the blink of an eye we complete a full turn and as my actions deflect the controls the horizon suddenly reappears between the wings, frozen and absolutely level, as I intended. I can't help grinning to myself. It's coming right again.

Another glance reminds me that the last item on the card is a loop. I open the throttle and at 120 mph start pulling back, my cheeks heavy under the g-forces until I look out over the top wing as we float inverted, making tiny corrections to keep straight on the road. As the biplane dives out of the loop there is a satisfying thump as I hit my own slipstream from the start of the manoeuvre. At least I know that the loop was straight.

I glance at my watch. Time has telescoped as it always does when I'm practising aerobatics. It is still only fifteen minutes since I took off but it seems twice that long. There is time to climb back to altitude and try my sequence again.

As I climb I find myself whistling inaudibly against the roar of the engine. A session of aerobatics is very therapeutic. The petty worries of earthbound life are temporarily banished and problems are put in their proper perspective. Concentration is complete. Absorbed in the process of perfecting my flying technique I am constantly learning, although it is at times a humbling experience.

At three thousand five hundred feet I check that I am alone in the sky and begin this aerial ballet again. I am more relaxed this time and it seems as if the Pitts knows this. My hands are more co-ordinated as they orchestrate stick and throttle and the Pitts responds by performing more precisely as we twist and turn through the clear air, wings flashing in the sunshine. This is the best time. Some days all goes well on the first attempt. More often it is sheer hard work in this constant striving for perfection.

As I pull up from the loop at the conclusion of the sequence I curve back into level flight and turn to head back to Santa Paula. It's best to quit while you're ahead in aerobatics as the cumulative effects of the g-forces are very fatiguing and the Pitts is not tolerant of mistakes on landing. Nose down and with wind wailing through the wires the biplane loses altitude, heading back towards the field which nestles at the foot of a rugged mountain crag.

As the grey ribbon of the runway slides past below the left hand wingtip I peer over the side to check the wind direction from the windsock. Satisfied that the wind is from the west and that there is no other traffic to hinder my approach, I bank to the left above the field, curving round until the mountain slides across my windscreen and I am heading east again. Keeping one eye on that mountain wall uncomfortably close to my right wingtip, I fly parallel to the runway, slowing down to 85 mph. Opposite the end of the runway I bank left again and start to curve round towards the runway, throttled back now and beginning to descend. Only by flying this curving approach will I be able to keep the runway in sight on my final approach, when the bulbous white engine cowling will dominate my forward vision. The runway at Santa Paula is short and narrow. Parked aircraft are arrayed on either side and power lines lurk in wait just short of the runway for the unwary flyer. It helps to keep the runway in sight.

From here on in things get busy. My eyes alternate between the fast approaching runway and the airspeed indicator. '. . . Keep that speed exactly on 85 . . . (too fast and I'll never stop on this short runway, too slow and both the Pitts and I will arrive abruptly on the ground) . . . keep it turning . . . a touch of power as we start to sink . . . speed 82 . . . nose down a touch . . . correct with stick and rudder as the wind drifts me off to the side . . . speed 87 . . . nose up a fraction . . . over those power lines . . . nearly there . . .'

As I level out, the white lines marking the edges of the narrow runway slide out of sight behind the engine cowling. I can do no more than look ahead and keep the wings level for a long instant of time. Out of the corner of my eye I see a flash of white and I ease back on the stick and throttle.

The tailwheel brushes the ground and the main wheels touch with a thump. The Pitts has a mind of its own on the ground and my feet are kept busy on the pedals, keeping the biplane straight on the runway until its speed drops to walking pace. I turn off the runway and taxi back, braking to a halt at the gas pumps. The engine coughs into silence and as I slide the canopy open the afternoon breeze, cool and fresh, sweeps into the cockpit.

The line boy drags the gas hose across to the Pitts.

'Nice day,' he says conversationally, opening the fuel cap and starting to fill the gas tank. I nod my assent, trying to bring myself back to this earth-bound existence. Words are inadequate to express the joy of flying this machine on such a perfect day. I slowly unstrap the seat harness and climb stiffly out of the cockpit, ears still buzzing from the racket of the engine. I step down to the ground, unbuckle the parachute harness and find that I am grinning.

'Yes, I guess you're right. It's a very nice day.'

2

The Sky Above

The desire to fly has been inherent in man for aeons. Only in the twenti-
eth century has the technology permitted sustained manned flight. The
variety of flying machines designed and built since the Wright brothers is
awesome and is a fascinating story in itself. My own path to the skies of
California encompasses two decades of flying a large variety of aircraft, hard
work and, incidentally, a lot of fun.

I grew up in England in the years after the Second World War. We lived
on the outskirts of Liverpool, a sprawling seaport at that time still recovering
slowly from the devastating effects of the Luftwaffe blitz. Playgrounds in the
city were largely confined to roughly-cleared bomb sites. However bad the
conditions underfoot, to a young and impressionable boy the sky above was
a constant source of wonder, with the roar of powerful piston engines or the
whistle of jets echoing down from the vault of the sky.

There was good reason for this. Within twenty miles or so were located a
variety of military airfields: the Royal Naval Volunteer Reserve flew
Supermarine Attackers from Stretton, while the Royal Auxiliary Air Force
operated Meteors out of Hooton Park. Most weekends a Meteor would wail
overhead towing a banner target. He would fly down the Mersey estuary en
route for gunnery practice out over the sea. Some time later the Meteor
would return, usually with a rather tattered banner.

From the East the big WB-50 Superfortresses of the USAF Weather Recce
Squadron at Burtonwood droned out over our house, flying out over the
Atlantic every day. Occasionally visits to Burtonwood by units flying the even
noisier B-36 varied this routine. On other occasions the B-36s boomed over
at forty thousand feet, drawing a spectacular swathe of contrails through the
heavens as they targeted Liverpool on their radar bomb runs.

My father took me for my first flight in a Fox Moth from Southport sands
at the age of ten. The cabin held four passengers in a noisy, cramped and
vibrating environment, with the pilot in an open cockpit to the rear of the
cabin. The discomfort was forgotten as we lifted off the sands. This was fun.
This was the place to be.

On my fourteenth birthday I joined the Air Training Corps. As a branch
of the RAF Volunteer Reserve, the ATC taught its cadets in Theory of Flight,
Navigation and Weapons, took them on summer camps to operational RAF
stations and did a host of other good things. But from my point of view the

icing on the cake was the fact that Cadets had the opportunity to fly in Chipmunks and could qualify for glider training. I worked diligently through the qualifying exams so that when the time came round I was ready to start glider training.

My glider training started at RAF Hawarden with 631 Gliding School. Hawarden was a ferry ride away across the Mersey. Bill Gray was the Commanding Officer of the School. We first flew in the side-by-side T21 Sedburgh, then progressed to the tandem-seat T.31. My instructor, Ken Higgins, was one of that breed of leather-lunged instructors who could berate cadets unmercifully from the open rear cockpit of the T.31 glider above the howl of the wind. Our gliders were towed up to altitude by an ex-barrage balloon winch. The sound of the instructor bellowing at his pupil at the top of the launch, when heard from the ground, was enough to give any young cadet second thoughts about embarking on this venture. Nevertheless we half-dozen neophytes embarked upon our first familiarisation rides.

On our first few trips we just flew around the circuit, with the occasional 360 degree turn thrown in for good measure as our confidence increased. We grew more accurate in our landings, a blessing for the other cadets who had to push the glider back to the launch point again. On a hot summer day, wearing the heavy RAF issue serge uniform, this was an unwelcome chore.

After I had mastered the basics of flying, Higgins had me practise simulated cable breaks just after lift-off. Having coped successfully with these, I was not unduly surprised when instructor Dave Westaway gave me the required independent pre-solo check. After we landed he climbed out and informed me casually that the next one I could do on my own.

By now it was late afternoon on a hot summer day. The T.31 rested wing-down on the grass while the tractor noisily pulled the cable back from the winch at the far end of the field. Time for the butterflies in the stomach to take wing. After the tractor dropped the cable, three of my fellow cadets pulled the heavy cable with its parachute across to the nose of the glider. At a nod from me the cadet at the wingtip heaved the wingtip off the ground. With wings level I automatically went through my checks, which Higgins had laboured hard to instill in me. Controls free . . . instruments . . . just the airspeed, altimeter and the red and green balls of the Cosim variometer to check . . . spoilers actuated and then locked in . . . trim OK . . . The T.31 required no ballast when flown solo, unlike the blunt-nosed Sedburgh irreverently dubbed the Barge. The cable release was checked.

Thus assured that I would be able to release from the winch, the cadet at the nose attached the cable again, gave it a heave to reassure himself of its security, and stood back a few paces, sweating profusely and with a broad grin on his face. We all took turns at these chores. They all knew by the empty rear seat that I was to take to the sky alone.

I tugged my straps tight and glanced over my shoulder. That rear seat looked really empty. Despite my dry throat I somehow sang out, 'Take up slack.'

Another cadet holding a pair of round bats signalled to the distant winch, shimmering in the heat haze at the far end of the field. There was a moment of delicious anticipation as the cable, lying in an arc on the grass, began to tighten, scything the long grass with a quiet swishing sound. When the cable arrowed towards the winch all was ready.

I shouted, 'All out.'

The waving bats relayed the message to the far end of the field. A puff of smoke drifted away from the winch and with a jerk the glider started to accelerate, soon out-distancing the cadet running at the wingtip. Now the ailerons were responding and the glider lifted, touched briefly and rose into the air. The parachute on the cable now billowed below the nose. My senses were alive. The cable was creaking, the wind wailing and strange noises came from the hook mechanism beneath my feet as the tension built up in the cable.

I started to pull back on the stick. The nose crept higher until the pitot probe vibrating in front of the windscreen was well above the horizon. As the altimeter read 600 feet, the glider started bucking against the tension on the cable and I realised that I was pulling back too hard on the stick. Easing forward into level flight, I was conscious of the wind howling as the speed increased. I pulled the release knob. There was a bang as the hook released and the noise diminished.

I was flying.

Everything was very peaceful and quiet. The view was superb from the open cockpit. Across the river lay the Cathedral at Liverpool. Ahead lay the sea and to my left the Welsh mountains were now backlit in the afternoon sunlight. But there was no time to waste in sightseeing. Training took over and I gingerly banked round, flying along the perimeter of the field as I gradually lost altitude. Another turn onto downwind, then again onto base leg. Making my final turn and pushing the nose down I increased the speed in case of gusts at low altitude. Now the grass started to blur as I came lower. The other parked gliders with the watching knot of cadets were clear of my path, away to my left. Out with the spoilers to kill the speed. The T.31 floated, light without the instructor's weight. The tailskid whispered through the grass, then the glider touched down on the single wheel, rumbling along until one wing dropped as the glider came to rest.

I unfastened my harness and clambered out shakily as the other cadets clustered round the machine. I was grinning from ear to ear.

Flying. It was pure magic.

3
The Mighty Mosquito

Over fifty years have passed since R.E. Bishop's team designed the de Havilland Mosquito, an unarmed bomber powered by two Rolls-Royce Merlins. The airframe was made mainly of wood to conserve strategic materials. During four years of combat, the Mosquito proved to be one of the fastest of contemporary aircraft. It was successfully developed as a fighter, a bomber and as a recce aircraft, was flown from aircraft carriers and was even pressed into service as a high-speed airliner in BOAC colours, carrying passengers in the bomb bay between Britain and Sweden.

In the spring of 1963 United Artists planned to make the film *633 Squadron* starring Mosquitos in a re-creation of Fred Smith's novel about a fictitious Mosquito squadron tasked with attacking a heavy water factory in Norway. Eight Mosquitos were finally located to serve in the movie. Five came from the Civilian Anti-Aircraft Co-operation unit at Exeter, two came from the Royal Air Force and one from private owner Peter F.M. Thomas. The flying sequences were handled by Captain John Crewdson's Film Aviation Services at Bovingdon, an RAF station just outside London, and on location in Scotland.

By the time the film appeared on the horizon I was writing occasional aviation articles on a freelance basis. When John Crewdson offered me the chance to come and fly in a Mosquito during the making of the film I needed no second bidding. So one blazing hot day in an English summer I found myself taken back in time as I passed through the main gate at Bovingdon.

Crewdson introduced me to the pilots. We briefed for the flight. I was to fly in Mosquito T.T. 35 TA639 with Flying Officer C. Kirkham from Royal Air Force Little Rissington. Kirkham would be the leader of Red Formation. The other two Mosquitos making up Red Formation would be another T.T. 35 flown by Flight Lieutenant D.J. Curtis. The third aircraft was a Mosquito T.3 flown by J.R. 'Jeff' Hawke, an ebullient ex-RAF Lightning pilot who was later to ferry two of the Bf 108s used in the film over to the USA. I would be taking photographs from the right hand seat of Red Leader. Our formation would consist of these three aircraft only. The resulting camera shots would be multiplied by the film technicians to give a full squadron of twelve aircraft.

At the end of the line loomed our Mosquito. While Kirkham carried out the pre-flight check I struggled into my parachute harness. The sheer size of the machine made pre-flighting difficult as the engines and spinners were way above our heads. The hydraulic pump handle was extracted from the bowels of the cockpit and rattled along the exhaust stubs of the Merlins to check their integrity, a latter-day version of the railroad wheel tapper's hammer.

With pre-flight checks completed I followed Kirkham up through the hatch in the belly of the Mosquito. There was only room for one person to move in the cockpit at one time. Encumbered with 'chute harness, flying helmet and camera, I eventually managed to wriggle my six feet plus into the starboard seat. Once our ladder was stowed, the outer hatch was slammed shut by our ground crew, sealing us in the cockpit.

Our aircraft had been standing in the sun all day. Consequently it was abominably hot under the perspex canopy and we were soon sweating profusely. We cracked the clear-view panels open to entice a current of air through the cockpit. While I fiddled with my window, Kirkham commenced his pre-start checks. An external power trolley had already been plugged into the belly of the Mosquito and the starboard engine was primed.

Kirkham gave a thumbs up to the ground crew and clicked the ignition switches on, followed by the starter. The huge three-blade propeller to my right shuddered, stopped, and jerked into life again until the Merlin caught and burst into life with a thunderous blast of sound. Clouds of exhaust fumes swept in through the open clear-view panel. By the time I had closed and locked the panel the port engine was also running.

Kirkham contacted the tower, obtaining clearance for Red Formation to taxi to runway 04. Altimeters were set to a QFE of 993 millibars. With the power brought up, at 1,500 rpm brakes were checked. Slowly we moved forward and turned, brakes squealing, onto the perimeter track, leading the other two aircraft down to a disused runway where all three aircraft turned into wind to complete the run-up.

The pilots checked that the brakes were fully on. Now the throttles were advanced and at 3,000 rpm the thunder of the Merlins battered through my leather helmet, shaking the whole aircraft. I could see the grass flattening in a yards-wide swathe behind the other aircraft as they ran up. Now Kirkham cycled the pitch controls, checked the trims and switched the fuel boost pumps on. We had trouble contacting Red 3, who started on his internal batteries and whose transmissions were rather weak at low rpms. Finally Kirkham checked the fuel panel, located awkwardly between and behind our seats. With checks complete we taxied round to the duty runway. The wind was calm.

Our Mosquito lined up with the other aircraft trailing us, propeller discs shining in the sun. Up to 3,000 rpm against the brakes. The noise and vibration were overpowering. A jerk as the brakes were released and we started moving. Jabs of differential brake kept us tracking straight as the Mosquito tried to swing to the left under the torque of the Merlins. At fifty knots the tail came up and the rudder was becoming effective. As we accelerated more rapidly the noise was undiminished but the vibration was lessening. At 110 knots the Mosquito lifted off, and at 130 the gear was folding itself majestically into the nacelles. We climbed straight ahead to two thousand feet and Kirkham throttled back to zero boost to maintain 150 knots at 2,400 rpm, then turned us gently to let the others catch up.

By now I was half-turned round in the bucket seat, craning to see rearwards to report on the progress of Red 2 and 3. As we turned through a lazy left hand circuit, the others gradually closed up behind us and took station with their wingtips level with our tailplane. I started taking photos again. With Red 3 aboard we tightened the turn and started to dive towards the field.

Speed drifted up to 220 knots as we tracked towards the camera crew out on the field. Bumping in the turbulent air over the boundary fence we bottomed out of the dive at 250 feet and pulled up to an altitude of two thousand feet again. The radio squawked that the next run should be lower and steeper.

Down we went again, the slipstream wailing over the noise of the Merlins. The quartering sun picked out the colours in the roundels and squadron markings on the fuselage of the aircraft hanging just off our right side, turning the arc of the propellers into shimmering discs. I attempted to take some pictures of Red 3 during the dive and luckily managed to squeeze the release just before the onset of g-forces at the bottom of the dive pushed me firmly down into the seat. Once more we motored up into the quieter air, circling the field while we changed formation into echelon starboard as briefed. We were now ready for our third dive.

Now the tower called us to wait as the technicians had some unspecified problem on the ground. For five minutes we orbited over the peaceful English countryside. Through a transparent panel in the hatch below my feet I could see tantalising glimpses of cool rivers and ponds. My harness was damnably tight and the cockpit was still hot. On this heading the sun was a blinding disc in the sky ahead of the nose and we were slowly being roasted. We turned south and mercifully the sun was blanked off by our wingtip, leaving the black silhouettes of the other Mosquitos gently rising and falling against the blinding light.

The tower came back on the air: 'One more run, please, and make it closer.' Kirkham looked across at me and grinned. The other aircraft crept closer to our tail. I turned my head to the front as we started the dive to see the field framed in the windscreen. Kirkham reached up and wound on the rudder trim handle to keep us straight as the speed increased. Then the g-force was pulling hard on my camera as we bottomed out of the dive. The perimeter track whipped past underneath, the grass expanding and blurring. I had an overwhelming urge to pull my feet up. A hurried glance at the altimeter showed that it was registering a mere hundred feet. Our true altitude was somewhat lower. We flashed over the camera crew and pulled up smoothly to a thousand feet.

'That's all, Red Leader,' crackled the radio. We broke formation, preparing to make individual landings. The engine note took on a more strident note as the propellers were moved into fine pitch. Now at 2350 rpm, boost pumps were switched on and as we pitched out on to the downwind leg the flaps came down. Kirkham checked the brake pressures. As we drifted down through five hundred feet the audio horn blasted our eardrums until it was silenced by edging the throttles forward. We descended in a long left hand turn. Gear extension was marked by a slight nose-down pitch and an interminable wait before the gear locked down. At 120 knots we came round on to finals, calling 'Red Leader, Finals. Two greens.' We rumbled down finals to a wheel landing, with the usual Merlin ear-splitting popping and banging once the throttles were closed. Finally the tail dropped and we turned off the runway and swung into dispersal. Kirkham switched the booster pumps off and pulled the fuel cut-offs, and the slowing prop blades became visible until they jerked to a halt. Under our feet the hatch was opened and we climbed down the ladder, deafened and relishing the cool of the evening air. Our aircraft loomed over us, engines ticking as they contracted, the air shimmering over the burning exhaust stubs, with the smell of hot oil in the air.

This was the last of the big twin-engined piston fighters to see wartime service in the Royal Air Force. It was a privilege to fly in this old warbird – the Mighty Mosquito.

4

College Days

Southampton University was a revelation to someone from the industrial north of England. The campus was pleasantly situated on the outskirts of the town, with the countryside only minutes away. Students came from all parts of the country and had come to study both arts and sciences, which made for a very cosmopolitan student body. At that time the university was still small by modern standards, being barely 3,000 strong. This meant that teaching was still on a very personal level. I had made Southampton my primary choice because of the excellence of the Aeronautical Engineering course.

There was one other factor that I had considered. Southampton had a University Air Squadron. More than that, it was unusual in having an Engineering Branch in addition to the usual General Duties (Flying) Branch of the RAFVR. Being still passionately interested in flying, I wanted to join the UAS. However I was very aware that my medical records from a previous application to RAF Cranwell would still be on file in the Air Ministry. I was sure that if I applied directly for the Flying Branch, my application would be summarily dismissed because of the medical technicality (a minor visual defect) which had tripped me up before.

Although glider flying had proved that my vision was adequate for normal flying, the records were still in existence. So I applied to join the Engineering Flight of Southampton UAS. After all, Officer Cadets in the Engineering Branch were permitted orientation flights in the UAS Chipmunks. Being accepted into the UAS was the initial goal. The rest would be up to me.

Eventually the selections for the UAS were announced. I was lucky enough to be one of those selected for the Engineering Branch, and after a couple of regular rear-seat orientation flights I convinced the commanding officer, Squadron Leader Johnston, that I knew enough about the Chipmunk to be allowed to fly it as a regular student from the front seat. So by the spring of 1964 I was flying again, when the rigorous schedule of the engineering department permitted.

Now that I had been allowed to start flying from the front seat, life became much more interesting and of course demanding. My instructors were Flight Lieutenants Doug Brady and Phil Alston, who were sympathetic to my cause and in effect trained me up to the standard required for solo. At this point I applied for a special transfer from the Engineering Branch to the Flying

Branch, so that I could go solo and complete the flying course. Despite the CO pursuing this with some vigour, the medical people at the Air Ministry just quoted the facts shown in my original medical report and quashed the request.

Down again, but not yet out, I continued with my instructors' help through the rest of the syllabus, although all my flying was of necessity carried out dual to keep the situation legal. We progressed to formation flying and aerobatics, which had always appealed to me.

Aerobatics were practised over the Isle of Wight and the hours spent at this were a grounding in my later flying. The disciplined RAF training I am sure made a difference. My instructors were all experts at their craft and the Chipmunk was a superb aerobatic mount. We flew from the grass field at Hamble, which we shared with the College of Air Training who trained airline pilots for British Airways.

This flying was not without its humour. Our Chipmunks had cartridge starters. They also had two sets of ignition switches, one in the front, one in the rear. It was not unknown for an intrepid aviator, flying solo, to attempt to start without checking that the rear switches were on. The immediate result of pulling the starter ring in the front cockpit would be a loud bang from the cartridge, a weak twitch of the propeller, an asthmatic wheeze from the engine and a gout of grey-blue smoke oozing out from every chink in the engine cowling. The red-faced cadet caught out in this way was then privileged to drink the traditional yard of ale at the next squadron meeting by way of penance. Our evening meetings, together with formal social occasions, were held in the imposing Headquarters Building down on the waterfront in Southampton.

It was all good fun. But I could see that the Ministry were unlikely to relent over my situation and so I sought an additional avenue to continue flying. Civil flying seemed to be out of reach on economic grounds. I only had the bare allowance of an impecunious student on which to exist. However, during my first term I had come across an exuberant flying enthusiast named Pete Tanner who was a professor in the Sound and Vibration Institute, part of the Engineering Faculty at the university. Peter was also the President of the Wessex Flying Group, which operated a Tiger Moth from Thruxton airfield. The method of group operation meant that the group members did a lot of the maintenance chores themselves, thus keeping the flying cost down to a fraction of the rate charged commercially.

So I promptly scraped up enough money to buy my required small share of the aircraft. I by now had obtained a student pilot's licence (the civil eyesight requirements not being as exacting as those for military flying) and started spending a greater proportion of my weekends flying the Tiger Moth. Once summer exams were over, I managed to wangle myself into summer camp with the General Duties Flight of the UAS who were going to Bicester to fly their Chipmunks. (Coincidentally Bicester was where the RAF Gliding & Soaring Association operated. I had flown with them before.)

Bicester was fun. It had a grass airfield which the Chipmunks shared with the gliders. After work was done for the day I would fly in the T.21s. On Wednesdays – RAF sports afternoon by tradition – we had the afternoons free. Rick Bishop, son of de Havilland designer R.E. Bishop, was a fellow squadron member and had somehow contrived to arrive at camp in a Hornet Moth. One busy Wednesday afternoon we flew in the Hornet Moth down to Thruxton, where I flew the Tiger Moth, then flew the Hornet Moth back to Bicester. I rounded off that very satisfying day by glider flying until the sun went down.

Due to academic and other conflicting interests, that year passed with little opportunity for flying. My Tiger Moth flying was restricted by persistently bad weather during the winter and Thruxton was closed down on more than one occasion by its proximity to A&AEE Boscombe Down, where the TSR2, the newest strike bomber for the RAF, was due to make its first flight. Invariably this happened on Saturday just as we wheeled the Tiger Moth out of the hangar, and invariably the day proved to be fruitless as the TSR2 failed yet again to fly and our day was lost.

It was not until the summer vacation when a course on Performance Flight Testing at the College of Aeronautics at Cranfield promised something new. Cranfield lay in the depths of Bedfordshire and was the very opposite of the university town atmosphere of Southampton. We flew in a pair of twin-engined Doves which the College had modified extensively for flight test work. This was interesting flying, as the Doves were flown about with trailing static bombs, covered in wool tufts to allow us to study airflow behaviour, and generally subjected to all kinds of indignities. I learned a lot from this intensive course.

Two days after the flight test course had finished, I was off with the UAS to summer camp in Malta, droning over Europe in an Argosy. We stayed at RAF Luqa to see how the RAF operated abroad, with a side-trip to Tripoli to visit the USAF base at Wheelus Field, with F-100s and F-105s thundering off at all hours and the oppressive heat of the north African night making it difficult for anyone to sleep.

In the summer of 1966 I graduated from Southampton with an engineering degree in Aeronautics and Astronautics. I was very conscious of knowing very little about the practical side of aircraft design and had determined that my next step would be to go to Cranfield to complete the two-year postgraduate course in aircraft design. I was accepted at Cranfield on the course which was due to start in September. During the summer I joined A&AEE at Boscombe Down, working as a flight test engineer on the operational acceptance trials of the Andover transport. We flew day and night in this intensive operational assessment of the aircraft.

At summer's end I packed yet again and drove my trusty Morris 10 to Cranfield. The College of Aeronautics had a famed reputation in aviation circles. David Keith-Lucas by now had moved from Short Brothers in Belfast and was our Professor of Aircraft Design, with Denis Howe as our Chief Academic Instructor. The reputation of the College was built on solid theory combined with practical experience covering the whole range of aircraft engineering. In the Department of Aircraft Design we had real aircraft on which we could practise. The Department of Flight, which operated the Doves, also had a French Morane-Saulnier MS 760 Paris jet for flight testing. The department also operated a Supermarine Swift, which was later replaced by a Hawker Hunter, for aquaplaning trials carried out on the main runway. To facilitate these trials the runway was criss-crossed by rubber dams which formed artificial lakes. Cranfield also had a gliding club and in addition the Department of Flight operated a training flight of Auster Aiglets. This was my idea of heaven.

I joined the Training Flight. Bert Russell was our Chief Flying Instructor. Bert was a moustachioed individualist who sported a monocle and was to be found with a tiny Jack Russell terrier permanently at his heels. Bert had flown everything from the College Lincoln, used for icing research, to the Shuttleworth Trust's Bristol Fighter and replica Avro Triplane which he used to fly on display days at Old Warden, the small grass airfield a few miles away. Bert was an intimidating figure on first acquaintance. His office had a complete shelf bulging with his logbooks. But once the ice was broken, Bert was revealed as an individual with a fine sense of humour.

We flew from the grass triangle between the runways at Cranfield. The Gliding Club operated on the far side of the runway. I briefly flew with the Gliding Club, but reluctantly had to give it up because of the time commitment required. It was much more convenient to fly the Austers at lunchtime and during any free periods I might have. So I concentrated on building up my flying hours and doing aerobatics out over the countryside at Olney.

Breaks in the generally gloomy weather provided me with some really spectacular flying. One sparkling spring morning I climbed between towering cumulus clouds to six thousand feet, where it was so cold that my breath was condensing in the cabin. From this lofty perch I could see as far as the balloon hangars at Cardington. I went through my small repertoire of aerobatic manoeuvres, culminating in a spin and then a falling leaf down to more normal altitudes. This was a welcome break from lectures. On another occasion I raced a thunderstorm back to the field, diving under the anvil and sideslipping down in a rising crosswind as a wall of rain advanced towards the field.

We had to keep our eyes open for other traffic in the air. Cranfield lay on a link route between the east coast USAF bases and Upper Heyford and we often saw sections of RF-101 Voodoos and the occasional KC-135 coming across the field just above circuit altitude. After a near miss when a section of RF-101s were forced to split to either side of a Cherokee as an avoiding manoeuvre, we all redoubled our vigilance near the field. During that summer we occasionally heard the radio crackle with strange messages from long ago: 'Spitfires – go. Watch out for the 109s. Go for the bombers.' Of course, this was the re-enactment of the Battle of Britain, now being fought out over the English countryside for the benefit of the film crews in the preparation of the film of the same name. Much of the flying was done over and around Cranfield and Duxford. One day I happened to look down when flying over the airfield at Duxford to recognize, with an eerie feeling, a solitary Messerschmitt Bf 109 parked on the otherwise deserted airfield.

Academic work at Cranfield was all-embracing. As a class project the members on the aircraft design course each year completed a design of an unconventional aircraft, thus introducing them to the type of problems that would occur in industry or in the services (we had a number of military and foreign students on the course).

Theory was not everything, though. We used real aircraft to check our theoretical results. Sometimes we did this in the hangar, torturing the CF-100 to check the torsional stiffness of the wing, or flying in the Doves to check performance techniques. Flight testing had its moments of humour, such as the day in the Dove when we laboriously climbed up through numerous layers of cloud while pilot Ron Wingrove attempted to find some clear air for us to observe the behaviour of the wool tufts on the wing during stalls. During the climb through cloud the tufts had become saturated with moisture. By the time we found clear air at nine thousand feet we were above the freezing level and the tufts were frozen rigid on their metal masts.

I volunteered to do an extra flight test course on the little Paris jet, the four-seat Morane-Saulnier MS 760 operated by the Department of Flight for aerodynamic and handling work. This was quite absorbing, with the faster and more responsive jet widening our experience after the staid Dove. Sandwiched between our gruelling academic work, once a week we whistled off for a sortie in the Paris.

At weekends I still managed to fly the Aiglets. Now that I had a civil licence, I started flying my fellow students around on cross-country flights. Some of them wanted to be shown aerobatics. I obliged by performing my basic manoeuvres at a safe altitude. After watching an air show routine, a couple of us decided to try our hand at toilet roll chasing. I tried it alone the first time. Starting at five thousand feet I opened the window and tossed out a toilet roll. As it unfurled, my intention was to do a diving turn and cut the

24

roll as many times as possible with the propeller. I found it surprisingly difficult as the fluttering strip of paper would slide off to one side or the other as
the aircraft approached. It was only when I started paying attention to the
rudder, balancing the Aiglet carefully, that I started to cut the paper with the
prop.

I was rather pleased with myself when I landed, only to have Bert Russell
storm out of the flight office, moustache bristling, demanding to know what
the hell I'd been doing. Warned by the sight of the other flight students falling
about laughing as they peered round the door of the Flight Office, I kept
quiet while Bert, dog trotting along at his heels, strode past me to the aircraft.

I turned round.

About twenty feet of pink toilet paper was trailing behind the Aiglet,
having caught on the bracing wires of the tail unit . . .

5

Cranfield's Highest Classroom

A quiet background whine was the only noise in a small classroom where, in company with two other students, I was recording the indications given by a series of panel-mounted dials. With the last value written down, I clicked my microphone on to report: 'Readings complete.'

A patch of sunshine slid slowly across the panel. With a few seconds' grace before my next task I shifted slightly in the seat to ease the discomfort of parachute and seat harness and snatched a quick look away from the instruments.

Instead of the green lawns of the College campus, a limitless vista of cerulean blue surrounded us, with a floor of fair-weather cumulus nearly two miles below. In the foreground a scarlet wingtip, tipped by a silver fuel tank, dipped towards the earth as the aircraft turned.

For this was no ordinary classroom. This was Morane-Saulnier Paris G-APRU, a twin-jet four-seat trainer used by the Department of Flight at the College of Aeronautics at Cranfield to give practical flight experience to postgraduate students dealing with the Sciences of Aerodynamics, Aircraft Design, Electrical Engineering and Propulsion.

This spring day in 1967, the purpose of our flight was to determine the manoeuvring stability of the Paris and the effect of pulling various amounts of g-force. At twenty thousand feet the aircraft was turning to starboard to come back on a reciprocal track towards Cranfield. The run just completed enabled datum conditions to be measured at 300 knots in steady trimmed flight. Elevator angle and the setting of the adjustable tailplane, airspeed and our altitude had been measured. Fuel state had been noted so that weight calculations could be made subsequently and the A13 paper trace recorder had been run briefly to obtain the datum conditions and to enable a visual check to be made on its operation.

The Paris was now heading south, with the sun blazing down through the perspex canopy and throwing the instruments into sharp relief. Ron Wingrove, the department test pilot, was setting up the aircraft for the next run as we drifted over a layer of thickening cloud spreading from the southwest. The engines were whining at 20,000 rpm. Airspeed was steady on 300 knots and we were trimmed straight and level.

In the right hand seat next to the pilot, I was monitoring the flight instruments. Peter Cox and Colin Harris in the rear pair of seats were responsible for measurement of tailplane angle and elevator angle, and checking the stick force from the SFECMA-instrumented control column. They also had the controls for the A.13 recorder.

The extensive instrumentation fitted to this aircraft by the Department of Flight enabled the dials on the panel to read out specific parameters which could be changed depending on the test programme required. In this way, six parameters out of a total of thirteen were selected for display on the six panel-mounted micro-ammeters. The thirteen parameters for which circuitry was installed permanently in the aircraft included those needed to assess handling qualities and to measure performance.

A disembodied voice broke in on this small world. This was the radar controller at Bedford, informing us of conflicting traffic at nine o'clock. I looked left to see them, two Phantoms out of Alconbury, streaming smoke and climbing fast. In a flash they were past us and we were clear to begin.

Colin Harris in the left hand rear seat switched on the A.13 recorder. A green light on the control box started to flash, indicating that the paper was moving through the recorder. Operation of the recorder time-base was confirmed by a red light blinking twice per second. With both lights signifying that the system was functioning satisfactorily we heard the confirming message: 'Recorder on.'

Ron pulled the Paris up into a climb, leaving the throttles in the cruise position. The engine oil system on the Paris was not cleared for operation under negative g-force conditions. To ensure maintaining positive g-force Ron put the stick smoothly over, the port wing went down and we rolled past the vertical, still under positive g-force. We were now in a steep dive, aiming to pull out at our original trimmed condition of 300 knots and 20,000 feet.

As the wings came level the nose was pointed down towards the cloud deck. During the pull-out the accelerometer reading crept higher. We were breathing more heavily under the strain and the g-force made it difficult to write down the instrument readings, but the blinking lights confirmed that the recorder was working satisfactorily. The nose probe crept up past the horizon, pencils returned to their normal weight and the aircraft whistled up into the heavens again.

We repeated this roller-coasting exercise during a series of pull-outs at increasing values of g-force. The next step was to record the same parameters again, this time in level flight but using progressively tighter turns to achieve higher values of g-force. When this also had been completed, the Paris was twenty miles north of the field. It was time to return. Steering 190 degrees, we began the descent, airbrakes out and throttled back.. The last sunshine glinted off the starboard tip tank, the sun dimmed and was snuffed out as we slipped down into the cloud. Mist started to form on the canopy and only the faint hiss of the air conditioning system broke the silence.

We slid out of the clouds, Ron snapped the airbrakes in and eased the throttles forward to check our descent. The runway lights were glowing ahead and slightly to our right. At one thousand feet we ran in towards the field from the east, overhauling at a safe distance a CSE Twin Comanche from Kidlington practising an ILS approach. Over the centre of the field we entered the break to port, buffeting slightly as the airbrakes came out to kill our speed. One forty knots and the flaps and gear were lowered.

'Romeo Uniform. Finals. Three greens.'

We came out of the descending turn to whistle down a flat approach to the runway. A slight check back on the stick and the tyres squealed as we touched down. Mission complete. Total time of flight: twenty-five minutes. As we slowed, Ron switched the pressurisation off and opened the canopy to let in a blast of fresh air, spiced with Avtur fumes, as we turned off the runway and taxied back past the two Doves used for basic flight test work by the department.

Our day's work was not yet finished. While the aircraft was turned round for the next sortie, the trace from this flight was unloaded from the recorder for the results to be analysed and discussed. Another three students were already being briefed for their flight, to carry out the same exercise at a lower altitude. Instructors Harry Ratcliffe and John Quick were kept busy overseeing the various stages of this operation.

The room fell silent as we three students drank coffee while waiting for our trace to appear. Australian Dave Ferry, a pipe-smoking naval aviator, was quietly working at the back of the room at his records from the previous flight. Our crew today came from different backgrounds. Colin Harris was a Flight Lieutenant from the Royal Air Force. Peter Cox came to Cranfield from Hawker Siddeley Aviation, while I came straight from College.

Flight testing was a co-operative effort. The sortie just completed was but one chapter in a story which began some months previously when we were introduced to flight testing using the propeller-driven Doves. Techniques of measuring thrust and drag were taught. The Doves grew feathers, or rather wool tufts, to investigate airflow behaviour during stalling, and trailed static bombs around the sky to measure pressure errors. Slowly the mysteries of basic practical aerodynamics were revealed. Then we had progressed on to the Paris for investigation of the stability and control of an aircraft capable of flying both higher and faster than the Dove.

Dutch rolls were now seen in terms of lateral derivatives and time-vector methods rather than the mental image of the worse-for-wear Dutch sailor previously imagined. The configuration of the Paris was changed many times during this investigation. Flights were made with the tip tanks full of fuel, then with tanks empty, to vary the rolling inertia of the aircraft. In further investigations of longitudinal stability it was a case of: 'An aft c.g. to be measured today. Can we have the two heaviest students in the back seats,

28

please.' Ballast weights were installed on some flights. For the next stage of flying they were taken out again if the schedule demanded it.

Many graphs were plotted and slowly the aircraft's flying characteristics became clearer. At the end of this day's flying the results of the various tests would be combined to show how this particular aspect of aircraft stability was affected in practice by changes in airspeed and altitude. The effect of c.g. shift on stick force per 'g' would be calculated to ensure that reasonable stick forces resulted from all aircraft loadings within the given operational limits. The control circuit of every aircraft must be designed to prevent the pilot having to use two hands to pull out of a dive or conversely to allow him to overstress the aircraft.

Despite the camaraderie between the young students on the campus outside this room, here there was an underlying sense of purpose. Our training flights were academic exercises at this stage, but flying in the aircraft gave a lasting impression that these points on a graph represented hard physical facts. A miscalculation could mean the loss of a pilot or the aircraft. The history of flight testing has been written the hard way, with aircraft coming apart or slamming into the ground because of design deficiencies.

At last the paper trace was brought into the office. As slide rules came out and we started to decipher the wavering lines on the paper, the rising whine of the two Marbore turbojets outside the classroom told us that another flight was on its way. A minute later the Paris was airborne once more, climbing until it was lost from sight, leaving a dying whine from the jets echoing across the field as it embarked upon another sortie as Cranfield's highest classroom.

6

The Burning Blue

On graduation from Cranfield I joined British Aircraft Corporation at Warton in the north-west of England to work on fighter aircraft. Here at the forefront of aeronautical technology I would be using the techniques I had been acquiring throughout my time at College. It was a busy time, with lots to be learned about the task of bringing the complex aircraft to flight status, but initially the job kept me in the office. To add one more factor to an already hectic life, during this summer I got married and Clare and I started to settle down after too many years regularly commuting each term to our respective colleges. It was late in the autumn by the time I found time to start flying again. Luckily, Blackpool airport was only a few minutes away from the company airfield at Warton where I worked.

I started out by checking out in a Cherokee, so preserving marital harmony by taking Clare, my wife, flying on a sightseeing trip up to the Lake District. Although she had grown up in the north of England, this was the first time she had seen the countryside from the air. The view of the Lakeland Hills covered with a dusting of snow on a gin-clear day that winter was spectacular. In the warmth of the cockpit the sight of a film of ice starting to form on Lake Windermere was beautiful, and a little eerie in the afternoon sun.

Then again there was the Chipmunk. G-ARGG was a civilianised Chipmunk, one of the few in the north of England. This example was owned by Air Navigation and Trading (invariably known as ANT) at Blackpool airport. It had an electric starter instead of the cartridge starter of the military version, but was otherwise identical to the military Chipmunks I had been flying two years previously. So again I started flying aerobatics. Once again I came to terms with the ground handling of this spirited machine, battling with those cantankerous differential brakes and juggling the sports-car-like brake lever on the left-hand wall of the cockpit while pushing on the rudder pedals to keep straight in the perennial gale-force winds at Blackpool.

Aerobatics in the Chipmunk were much easier than in the Auster Aiglet and I soon got back into practice. The Chipmunk was a perfect vehicle to indulge any Walter Mitty fantasies. The front cockpit was spartan but bore a striking resemblance to that of a Spitfire. A sliding hood, stick and tailwheel completed the fighter-like arrangements. In fact the Battle of Britain Memorial Flight checked their pilots out on Chipmunks before letting them loose on their Hurricane and Spitfire piston-engined fighters. In the air the

Chipmunk's handling was superb, and the ground handling with the tail-wheel was sufficiently interesting to make sure that the pilot kept awake during the landing roll.

As time went on I realised that the weather in the north of England was much more treacherous than down in the south, where I had done most of my flying. There were mountains to the west of us in Wales, to the east the Pennines ran down the spine of England and to the north were the hills of the Lake District. Very spectacular on a sunny day, but those days were the exception, especially during the winter months. I had not done much recent instrument flying and it appeared that one day the marginal weather would turn really bad on me.

Jane Murdoch offered to do some instrument flying with me. Jane was an instructor at ANT and I had met her the previous year when we had both attended a Light Aircraft Design course at Rearsby. Now Jane took time off from flying a Stampe biplane at displays while I learned again how to fly the Chipmunk on instruments.

The method used in instrument training was straight out of the fifties. The system had been called two-stage amber by the Royal Air Force. Amber screens were fitted on the inside of the front cockpit and windscreen. The student under instruction wore blue goggles. The result of this was that the outside world was completely obscured, while the interior of the cockpit was still visible. In the Chipmunk, with only a single radio, approaches into Blackpool were either laborious VHF Direction Finding (VDF) letdowns, with the tower giving bearings, or on rare occasions full radar letdowns which were much simpler. In a spirit of devilment, Jane used to talk me all the way through a simulated GCA down to an actual three-point touch-down. This was an act of faith on her part but magically we always ended up with the wheels rumbling down the runway.

When I had my rating, I used to delight in climbing up through the winter murk in the Chipmunk, with the narrow cockpit quiet, all the instruments giving their proper indications and only grey cloud outside. Moisture streaked back across the screen as I climbed. Three thousand feet . . . four thousand feet . . . with the Gipsy Major purring away serenely until the cloud lightened miraculously and the Chipmunk burst out into the cold clear world of limitless blue which only aviators could find.

For the first few seconds there was always a great impression of speed because of the nearness of the blinding white of the cloud-deck whipping past only feet below the wings. It was always cold in the Chipmunk, with the heating arrangements being primitive and largely ineffective at five thousand feet. Despite the discomfort it was always hard to throttle back and descend into the winter gloom again, knowing that the burning blue was waiting above the clouds.

7

Flight Testing

The Flight Test Department at British Aircraft Corporation's Military Aircraft Division at Warton was a busy place. Flight testing was enjoyable, if hectic, as I had acquired a taste for this aspect of the design process during my Cranfield course. At that time Roland Beamont was the Director of Flight Operations; Jimmy Dell was Chief Test Pilot and D.R.H. Dickinson was my boss in flight test. My initial tasks were concerned with stability and control trials on the later versions of the Lightning, but I was also intermittently involved in experimental and production flight testing on the Jet Provost.

Production test flying was another addition to my experience. I had never really considered the final product in practical terms. Once the aircraft was designed, it went into manufacture. At this stage surely the aircraft just rolled from the production line one after another like peas in a pod?

That was a mistaken assumption on my part. Each aircraft seemed to have its own idiosyncrasies, depending on the tolerances of the thousands of parts used in its manufacture. The production shop had the task of fine-tuning the aircraft as they came off the line so that they all behaved in the prescribed manner. Production flight testing was the means by which this was achieved.

My initial flying as a flight test engineer was done on Mk 4 Jet Provosts, undergoing acceptance checks after refit and destined for the Royal Air Force. Originally manufactured by Hunting Percival, the single-engined Jet Provost was a pleasant enough jet trainer which had its ancestry in the piston-engined Provost which appeared just after the second world war. It had survived the conversion to jet power quite well and RAF pilots from the fifties onwards had started their careers on the various early versions of the Jet Provost. However, high altitude navigational sorties in RAF service revealed that the students and instructors were being exposed to the bends, a painful condition of the joints caused by rapid pressure differentials, a problem exacerbated by the unpressurised cockpits of these early versions.

The Jet Provost Mk 5 was the logical solution to this problem, being modified to incorporate a pressurised cockpit. Warton had inherited the Jet Provost project when Hunting Percival had been taken over by British Aircraft Corporation.

Most of the design work had been completed at Luton, with Hunting Percival, and two prototypes, XS230 and XS231, had been built. By 1968

32

both prototypes had been moved to Warton. The pressurised cockpit was a fairly major change to the aircraft. This new cockpit gave the aircraft a more streamlined but more bulbous look around the front end, and the changed airflow altered the handling characteristics to such an extent that a flight test programme was required to re-examine the stalling and spinning characteristics of the aircraft.

It was cheaper to fly the prototypes than to embark upon an expensive wind tunnel testing programme. So a prototype was extensively tufted and flown with a Cessna 172 chase plane taking photos of the tuft movement during low-speed flight so that the airflow patterns near stall speed could be established. The flight test engineer took a mirror with him so that he could check on the flow on the fuselage behind the cockpit. There was a good deal of work in perfecting new wing root fairings, which came from Warton's own fibreglass shop. But eventually a suitable fairing shape was found and the flow was tamed.

Spinning was another problem. Whereas the spinning behaviour of the earlier Jet Provosts had been conventional, on the Mk 5 Jet Provost the spins tended to become oscillatory. The oscillations in pitch gave a very uncomfortable and disorienting ride. Our prototypes were pressed into service to test a number of modifications to calm the spin. During this phase of testing, pilot Reg Stock and Flight Test Engineer John Scutt set a record by carrying out no less than thirty-two separate spins during one sortie. Their tenacity was rewarded. With a number of aerodynamic modifications added, the spinning behaviour was tamed, the aircraft was cleared for RAF use and examples started rolling off the production line. It was at this time that I flew on my first production check ride with a Jet Provost 5.

The walk across the ramp from the flight test building seemed endless as I walked out to Jet Provost Mk 5 serial XW364. In addition to my flying kit I was laden down with helmet, life preserver, kneepad and stopwatch, together with a spring balance so that the aileron forces could be checked in flight. This aircraft was still in its factory finish with serial markings stencilled on the pale green primer paint. It had already flown once and I had noted that a few snags were recorded on its first flight, with an adjustment of aileron trim, to even out the aileron forces, being one of the items to be checked on Flight 2.

Pilot Reg Stock joined me at the aircraft and conducted a careful pre-flight inspection while I strapped into the right hand Martin-Baker ejection seat, which would blast me clear of the aircraft if things went wrong. Reg bantered with the ground crew while I strapped in. The Martin-Baker seat in the Jet Provost was one which I could never come to terms with from the comfort point of view. With my six foot plus frame I usually ended up with the seat fully down so that my helmet did not hit the canopy. Reg quickly strapped into the left hand seat and we went through the ritual of taking out the various ejection seat safety pins. The seats were now live. I stowed the pins in a rack on the cockpit wall. We were ready for business.

Reg completed his pre-start checks and hit the starter button. Way behind us the wail of the Viper turbojet rose in pitch, while I concentrated on timing the engine acceleration as it whined up to idle rpm. It was a grey and overcast day, and a chill wind blew through the cockpit. Only when Reg closed the canopy did things become a little more comfortable. I was busy checking off the items on my schedule for the production acceptance flight. These minutiae were the reason for Flight 2 and we had a busy time ahead.

We taxied out and backtracked to the head of runway 09, turning until the nose pointed down the grey strip of the runway. I made a final check of the oxygen, with the mask pinching my cheeks and the oxygen doll's eye blinking on the panel. We were both ready to go. Reg advanced the throttle to full power. The rpm stabilised and I took the rpm and jet pipe temperature readings. When I had finished, I nodded across the cockpit to Reg and as he released the brakes I started my stopwatch.

Acceleration to take-off speed in this jet was smooth, with none of the commotion of a piston-engined aircraft. We lifted off and were almost immediately in cloud, climbing under radar direction and already turning left towards our test area over the Irish Sea. I was busy writing, so absorbed in recording engine parameters and elapsed times each five thousand feet that only the sudden appearance of sunlight on the panel told me that we had broken through the overcast. We were climbing smoothly north-westwards with the Viper whistling like a vacuum cleaner somewhere behind us. Despite the apparent lack of effort, we were already climbing through twenty thousand feet in the time it would have taken my Chipmunk to climb to five thousand. But then a discordant note appeared. As we climbed through twenty-five thousand feet a gentle but persistent fore-and-aft thrust pulsing showed that one of the engine controls which compensated for the changing altitude would need a minor tweak before the next flight. I noted this down, and as we continued to climb the thrust pulsing died away.

At thirty thousand feet we levelled out and I snatched a glance out to see the coastline rimming almost the whole of the Irish Sea, with England, Scotland, Ireland and Wales all visible in the distance, while below us the perfect outline of the Isle of Man lay in the sea some six miles below. We slowly turned south, and off to our left our own fading condensation trail marked our climb path through the sky. During our cruise southbound we checked the radios and navigation gear, contacting in turn the various radio stations out to maximum range. Everything checked out with a clean bill of health.

We were ready for the next item on our checklist, a dive to the limiting

Mach number to check handling. Reg eased the nose down and we accelerated until the Machmeter reached the required figure. Occasionally an aircraft would start buffeting or pitching at high Mach as the local flow went supersonic over part of the airframe, giving the crew a graphic demonstration of transonic aerodynamics, but this aircraft gave no problems at all and we pulled back up to altitude.

We continued to the next part of the acceptance schedule: spinning behaviour. As the throttle came back to idle, a touch of airbrake slowed us further, with some buffeting as the airbrakes came out. Then the buffeting faded away as the airbrakes retracted. As we approached the stall Reg applied full rudder. The little jet yawed, rolled over onto its back and started spinning. I rather enjoyed spinning and religiously counted off the turns as we did this first spin to the right and then recovered. No problem in either the spin or the recovery and we climbed back and repeated the spin to the left this time. There were no abnormalities in either the spin or the recovery. Another item was duly checked off on my list.

It was time to check those aileron spring forces to see if the adjustment by the ground crew after the first flight had been successful. I passed the spring balance to Reg. As he pressed the balance against the stick, to give full stick deflection, the Jet Provost obediently started a smart roll through 360 degrees. We were absorbed in checking the figures, quietly conversing between the two of us, oblivious of the fact that outside the cockpit the world was rotating rapidly. The balance gave a figure that was within limits so we repeated the roll in the other direction, getting a similar reading from the balance. No bugs in the control system now.

During a routine check of the fuel quantity, I flicked the switch between tanks only to get a zero fuel indication. This was enough to catch anyone's attention. In a single-engined jet out over the water as we were at that moment this could have been serious. However the engine kept running and we decided that it was probably an electrical snag. A reselection of the switch miraculously brought back our fuel.

By this time we were coming back in over the coast. During our flight the clouds had burned off over the land and we found a clear patch to carry out our required high speed dive to 450 knots. This meant diving steeply at fairly low altitude. Admittedly this was not my favourite phase of a flight, strapped passively in the right hand seat as we hurtled down into the bumpy air at this impossibly steep angle with the fields expanding all round us. Then I was straining to resist the g-force as Reg pulled out of the dive and coasted up to ten thousand feet again. No problems there.

We now checked the landing gear and flap system operating times. Occasionally the gear might be sluggish, or a door might not close properly. On this aircraft everything was within limits. During this time Reg Stock had been keeping a close watch on our position. Our home field at Warton now lay off the left wingtip and we were ready for our next check, an engine shutdown and restart. A prudent pilot always would be near enough to reach base in the unlikely event of the relighting of our single engine not being successful. Reg pulled the throttle back and stopped the engine. We glided silently for a while with the airflow whispering eerily over the canopy before he restarted the single Viper and it wailed back into life.

By this stage of flight my kneepad was always full of scribbled notes and reminders. It was just this attention to detail which was required to produce a successful aircraft. Each item might seem of small significance, but there is precious little room for error in the world of flying, especially when this aircraft would be flown by fledgling aviators for most of its service life. Perfection is demanded and this aircraft would be delivered in a perfect state.

That concluded the production schedule. We returned overhead base with a break on to the downwind leg, curving round on a fighter-type approach down the runway. When the brakes were applied I felt some brake judder shaking the aircraft as the aircraft slowed on the runway. Reg shook his head. This meant another flight would be required after the brakes had been fixed. I noted the snag for rectification.

On the whole, 364 was not a bad ship. It would take one more flight to iron out those problems from the flight just completed. Then the aircraft would be wheeled into the paint shop to emerge in its smart red and white RAF training colours. By the following week an RAF pilot would arrive at Warton and ferry it to its new home, joining the training fleet.

Production testing was just one of the responsibilities that Flight Operations and Flight Test had in the overall organisation.

This was a time of transition, when experimental flight testing was moving away from the use of the paper trace recorders and notepads that had been the means of noting down the aircraft behaviour during trials. When I joined the department, my responsibility was to assess the directional stability of the Lightning during the supersonic flight trials that were under way on the Mk 6 and the Mk 53 and Mk 55 export Lightnings for Saudi Arabia. This was a serious concern. The Lightning trainer had suffered a couple of in-flight structural failures of the vertical fin during supersonic flight. The first had resulted in test pilot John Squier baling out and drifting about the Solway Firth in his dinghy for a couple of days before he drifted ashore.

After modification of the vertical fin all had gone well until Jimmy Dell and Graham Elkington had a somewhat similar fin failure during supersonic manoeuvring. Jimmy Dell, who had a fine sense of humour, said in later years that he always worried when flying with a Flight Test Engineer that the FTE would be so wrapped up in recording events that he would not realise that anything was wrong. In this case, Dell said, his fears were unfounded.

He heard three bangs in quick succession. The first was the fin failing, the second was the canopy being jettisoned and the third was Elkington ejecting, leaving Dell alone in the cockpit. Pausing only to give a quick 'Mayday' call, Dell pulled the ejection handle and ejected. They both drifted down under their canopies and were picked up from the Irish Sea.

With the advent of the Jaguar, and a requirement of carrying out a heavy flight test programme to clear the aircraft for both French Air Force and RAF service, a comprehensive system of recording data on magnetic tape was introduced. The most immediate result was a vast reduction in the turn-around time to analyse data between flights, and a huge increase in the number of parameters which could be patched in at short notice to investigate specific engineering or aerodynamic problems.

Production testing on the Jet Provost, the Lightning and the Jaguar was in some ways an anachronism, as the production aircraft did not have extensive instrumentation. It was more akin to flight testing in the old days, when it was largely the pilot's experience which determined if a potential problem existed. But production flight testing was a welcome break from the office and I found it very useful to keep in touch with the final product. The Jet Provost 5 was developed further into the Strikemaster light attack jet which is still in service at the time of writing.

8

Encounter with a Giant

Gliding in the north of England could be frustrating. There was only a handful of gliding sites within easy driving distance. Winter weather meant that the gliding season was short and generally confined to summer weekends. However this meant that there was plenty of time to watch the sky. From time to time I had seen tantalising glimpses of lenticular clouds over Lancashire. It struck me that these might indeed indicate a powerful wave system high in the sky.

My previous gliding experience had been primarily by using thermals or hill lift. I was well used to circling in a thermal, inching upwards with eyes glued to the variometer, trying to keep central in the rising air. Even in the sleek Blanik, success was not guaranteed, as British thermals were generally not as strong as those in warmer countries. Imitating the seagulls by using upcurrents in front of a hill could also keep you up for a respectable time but you were limited in the maximum altitude that could be reached.

During my college days sailplane pilot Max Stevens had shown slides of the wave systems in his native New Zealand that enabled record-breaking sailplane flights to be made almost routinely. The lenticular clouds I occasionally saw over Lancashire looked the same. Could we have waves in Lancashire? And would they be strong enough to use?

It was an intriguing thought.

Wave systems were strange. The combination of the right atmospheric conditions, wind and mountains could set the air oscillating many miles downwind of the hills, with the effects stretching to much higher altitudes than the hills themselves. Wave-soaring provided the glider pilot with a stepladder to reach heights that could otherwise only be attained within the turbulent interior of a cumulo-nimbus cloud. The world absolute altitude record for gliders had stood for many years at forty-six thousand feet, held by Paul Bikle flying in the Sierra wave in California. Even the modest Scottish mountains had produced height gains in the region of thirty thousand feet.

From my home in Preston, the Pennines to the east rose to barely 2,000 feet, while across the Irish Sea to the south-west the Welsh hills were topped by Snowdon at 4,000 feet. To the north the Lakeland hills also rose to four thousand feet. With this topography, I reasoned, wind from any direction might trigger some sort of a wave system, given the correct atmospheric conditions. Waves certainly were not impossible, as during my initial gliding from Sealand near the Welsh Border occasionally our Sedburghs had managed to connect with lift which could only have been part of a wave system.

My curiosity was aroused. Could I make a systematic investigation to see if usable wave lift existed in our area? The random nature of the wave system meant that it was not really feasible to play a waiting game at the glider fields. However, there was an alternative. I could use a powered aircraft to investigate any possible wave system. Using the Chipmunk I could get airborne from Blackpool within the hour. So I just had to be patient until the weather might indicate that a wave system was forming.

Throughout the early part of 1974 I played a waiting game, studying the weather maps and looking for any sign of the wave. On 25 April an unusual weather system with high pressure to the north resulted in a weak warm front advancing from the north-east, giving light rain over Lancashire in the afternoon. At five o'clock in the afternoon the sky began to clear and as the layer of stratus broke, a single bar of lenticular cloud appeared, stretching from north to south between Lancaster and Preston, maintaining position despite the easterly wind.

This looked like a good opportunity to check out my theories. I was airborne from Blackpool within the hour and as the Chipmunk climbed eastwards I could see two well-defined lines of multi-layered lenticular clouds which had now formed upwind of the original bar. As I climbed above the tattered layer of stratus that hung over the coast a further flat lenticular was revealed over the port wingtip, stretching southwards down the coast from Fleetwood. This thin veil floated at 6,000 feet, but there was no lift discernible in the immediate area.

Over the nose I could see the most spectacular cloud sitting over Preston. Its base was at 7,000 feet and the cloud rose in a stack of six pale grey saucers, linked laterally by bars of cloud to a similar stack. It was an awesome sight. Further north, towards Lancaster, I could see another stack of lenticulars partially visible, with the upper reaches lost in an ill-defined curtain of stratus. I could not climb over Preston because of the proximity of Amber One airway, so I decided to look more closely at the northern cloud.

Flying eastwards between these two towers of cloud, trimmed straight and level at 8,000 feet, I turned gently to port on to a northerly heading along the windward side of the lowest lenticular. Having heard stories of encounters with the dreaded rotor cloud associated with wave systems. I checked my parachute harness and snugged myself tightly into the seat. But initially nothing happened. I was puzzled. It looked like a wave system, but would the facts bear this out?

The air was smooth, but I suddenly noticed that the vertical speed indicator was indicating a 200 ft/min rate of descent. This was promising. Then the VSI flickered to show 200 ft/min climb. After a few minutes of this intermittent plus and minus 200 ft/min, the VSI swung solidly up to 500 ft/min rate of climb.

This was more like it.

As the northern edge of the cloud drifted past the port wingtip, the VSI swung further up until it was showing over 1,000 ft/min rate of climb, better by far than the normal rate of climb at full power. Yet here I was, still at cruise power, trimmed out and not putting any inputs into the stick at all.

This was indeed a respectable wave system. The lift continued as I turned downwind round the edge of the cloud, with my rate of climb tapering off until the needle hit zero, then as I emerged clear of the cloud the VSI started to show a growing sink rate. At nine thousand feet I could see that the Cock Hill gliding site, deserted on this weekday evening, lay almost underneath the southernmost stack of lenticulars.

It was frustrating to know that the proximity of the sea and of controlled airspace made it unlikely that any sailplane could use this wave system, but I was pleased that I had confirmed its existence. It might be months before conditions were right again for the wave to form, but I now knew that it was there.

Late into that evening, the lenticular clouds glowed eerily high in the sky, but the next day dawned to give a cloudless sky.

The wave had gone . . .

On another occasion, later that summer, the sun was glinting on a smooth sea as I climbed away from Blackpool airport for an evening session of aerobatics. A light south-westerly wind was enough to fill the sails of the yachts clustered in the Ribble estuary. The sky was peaceful, marred only by scattered patches of stratus at about 5,000 feet. My climb-out northwards along the coast was uneventful until abeam Blackpool Tower when passing through 2,500 feet the Chipmunk hit a patch of turbulence as I flew under a cloud. The motion was sharp-edged and random, fitting perfectly the characteristic 'cobblestone' description of clear-air turbulence. It was so unlike the normal convective turbulence that I began to suspect at once that this was some sort of rotor flow. But after a few seconds of jolting flight the air smoothed out completely.

As the Chipmunk passed out into the sunshine once more, I automatically scanned the instruments: airspeed seventy knots, engine temperature and oil pressure normal, vertical speed indicator zero . . . Zero? I performed a rapid double-take, but zero it stayed. The altimeter confirmed the situation. The Chipmunk was suspended in space, still in a climbing attitude with the Gipsy Major still putting out full power.

Suspicion was now hardening into certainty. I must be in the descending air of a mountain wave system, even though the nearest hills upwind of me were forty miles away in North Wales and the winds seemed too light to support the formation of a wave system. I turned downwind, tracking across the gap between two clouds and barely maintaining altitude. Approaching the upwind edge of the next cloud, I guessed that the air in the wave must start to rise again and I banked the Chipmunk round until I was flying parallel to the cloud.

I was watching the needle of the VSI like a hawk. After a few seconds the needle reluctantly left the zero mark, inched up to show a climb rate of 200 ft/min and then, as smoothly as the sweep hand of a clock, swung up to 800 ft/min rate of climb. The Chipmunk shot upwards like a champagne cork past the thin layer of cloud. As the altimeter passed 7,500 feet the rate of climb peaked at 1,000 ft/min, almost double the still-air rate of climb at this altitude. By 8,500 feet I levelled out and came back to cruise power. The aircraft was still rising at 400 ft/min.

At this height visibility was excellent and as I turned westwards an awe-inspiring panorama was spread out beyond the cowling. The whole of the Lancashire coast was visible, with the wave system's characteristic lenticular clouds forming at different heights. An irregular pattern of glowing bars of lenticulars at high altitude stretched westwards across the Irish Sea. Away to the north a stack of saucer-shaped clouds hung above more extensive cloud cover over the Lake District. Yet more saucers hung over the Pennines to the east.

In one sense it was a sobering thought. Had I been a few miles further east over the rising ground and in solid cloud, the torrent of descending air in the down-going side of the wave could easily have pushed the Chipmunk down into the hills.

But still the thought of the potential of using these waves niggled at me. On the soonest possible occasion I would try to use the wave in a glider. However, this was not to be. Within a few weeks I was to be plunged into the Tornado flight test programme, which left precious little time for the time-consuming sport of gliding. I wrote up my observations on these occurrences and they were published as articles in *Flight International* and *Sailplane and Gliding*.

That was all.

By the time the Tornado pressure had eased somewhat, I was involved even more deeply with powered aircraft, building an aerobatic biplane and it was to be some years later before I flew again in a glider in California. I only met up with the Lancashire wave one more time, flying a powered aircraft in instrument conditions, and I remember being exasperated beyond measure by an aircraft that insisted on climbing and descending with a will of its own, until I realised what was causing the problem.

From this flying I was left with a healthy respect for wave systems, and the knowledge that one day I might be able to make use of my experiences.

9

Farewell to England

I still found flight testing to be an exciting and spectacular environment. The Lightning, with its twin Avons in full reheat, had a performance which was years ahead of any other fighter, and Roland Beamont's practice demonstrations before each Farnborough Airshow were guaranteed to stop work in the flight test office for the duration of the demonstration as the Lightning scorched round inside the airfield boundary with both afterburners thundering. Lightning take-offs were similarly awesome, with the aircraft climbing almost vertically from the runway, balanced on a pair of yellow spears of flame studded with diamond shockwaves. Warton was busy with Canberras being ferried abroad, Lightnings being delivered to Saudi Arabia, and refurbished Lightnings being returned to the RAF.

Being responsible for aircraft handling led to some interesting projects. Spinning trials of the Mk 6 Lightning revealed that despite the sheer massiveness of the Lightning and its unconventional sixty degree swept wing, its spinning behaviour proved to be largely conventional. As with all heavy jets, the loss of altitude per turn was awe-inspiring, but recovery action worked every time. I spent many hours with aerodynamicist Sandy Burns incarcerated in a telemetry van parked out on the airfield while pilots Tim Ferguson and John Cockburn spun the big fighter.

But we started to break new ground with the Jaguar. The Jaguar had a number of innovations. It had been designed jointly by the French and British teams to satisfy a variety of requirements laid down by the French Air Force and the Royal Air Force. The various conflicting requirements sounded like a recipe for disaster. Intended to be an economical strike aircraft in a single-seater version, and a supersonic trainer in the two-seat version, the Jaguar had heavy-duty landing gear and full-span flaps to enable it to take-off from short grass fields.

Use of this flap system left no space for ailerons and roll control was necessarily by spoilers on the upper surface of the wing. The spoilers resulted in some idiosyncrasies in roll control being encountered during early flying and a lot of development time was spent on ironing out these problems.

Directional stability was initially inadequate and the vertical fin was enlarged, and ventral fins added under the rear fuselage. In company with other swept-wing jets, the Jaguar proved to have a wing-rocking problem if pulled hard into a turn. Autostabiliser modifications cured this.

If this sounds like a litany of disastrous proportions, it was not. These problems were encountered largely around the edges of the flight envelope and were typical of any aircraft under development. This was the reason for flight test. The Jaguar proved a very effective strike aircraft under programme manager Ivan Yates.

During the Jaguar design phase we had learned that North American had been carrying out spinning trials on their big A-3J Vigilante and had found that the big jet had a very oscillatory spinning mode. As the Jaguar similarly had a swept wing mounted high on the fuselage, it looked as if it might exhibit the same behaviour.

An extensive programme of wind tunnel model testing was carried out in the vertical tunnel at Lille in France, supplemented by free-flight model tests in England, where large models of Jaguars with controls preset to force the model into a spin were dropped from helicopters over the Larkhill range. The models spun beautifully.

Eventually the spinning trials were transferred to the full-size aircraft. Prototype M05, the French maritime Jaguar, was used for these trials, flying from Istres in southern France.

This meant that commuting in the company HS 125 down to the south of France became a frequent occurrence. Istres was the French Air Force test base, comparable with Edwards AFB in California, and was a veritable storehouse of strange prototype aircraft. Dassault were flying their variable sweep Mirage and the Mirage F1; the Mercure airliner and the Falcon.

At the working level the French and British Flight Test teams working on the Jaguar programme had co-existed profitably throughout the programme. French pilots flew our Jaguars, British pilots flew theirs.

Lunches at Istres took some getting used to however. We were invariably taken to a restaurant off-base for a leisurely and stylish lunch, complete with an unending supply of the best local wine. We learned to complete our business before lunch.

The main difference in technique between British and French methods of testing was the spinning trials. Whereas in England our spinning was done over uninhabited moorland, at this desert airfield at Istres the spinning trials took place directly over the airfield, starting at 45,000 feet, primarily to obtain good kine-theodolite coverage of the gyrations of the aircraft. It was an unsettling feeling to stand on the balcony of the flight test building and squint up directly overhead into the clear sky, where the sunlight flashing on the rotating aircraft showed the inexorable descent of the jet . . .

But all went well, and M05 recovered every time, although the predicted oscillatory spin was encountered and gave the pilots a rough ride before the aircraft recovered.

Jaguar testing went on apace, with many different stores combinations

44

being tested on the British and French prototypes. Jimmy Dell, Paul Millett, Dave Eagles and John Cockburn carried out the bulk of the flying. The Jaguar had a very sophisticated weapon aiming system for the time. Ultimately the aircraft entered RAF and French Air Force inventories as a successful strike aircraft. One of the last Flight Test Projects on Jaguar was to operate Jaguar S07 from the newly-constructed M55 motorway near Blackpool in a successful demonstration of its operating versatility, with Tim Ferguson the pilot on this occasion. The aircraft was landed on the road, refuelled, bombed up and dispatched back to Warton with no fuss at all.

By now Flight Test was gearing up for the Tornado. Again a strike aircraft, we again had the task of flying with a new turbofan engine, the RB199.

The first prototype flew in Germany, but the second and third prototypes flew from Warton. The Tornado brought an introduction to an even more complex aircraft. Flight test expanded again. Pilots and engineers all attended ground school to learn about the complexities of the aircraft. Testing went well, but the red and white prototype P02 was nearly lost when one of the engines swallowed a seabird as the aircraft was overflying the airfield during a planned low-speed trial. Pilots Millett and Eagles had a worrying few moments before they managed to accelerate away on the remaining engine and get back to a more reasonable flying speed.

We in Flight Test worked with all of the other departments and with Gary Willox, the Tornado programme manager. Each morning all department heads would meet to keep tabs on the previous day's progress and to be appraised of the progress of the tri-national programme. With flight testing and production simultaneously being carried out in Germany, Britain and Italy, just keeping track was a complex task.

Avionics prototype P08 became my primary responsibility and it was a different experience to monitor the bulk of the test flying from the ground. Now I sat at my console backed by a team of engineers, each member of the team in turn seated before a glowing console. With a multiplicity of sensors on the aircraft, we often had more depth of information available to us than the pilot. Now we could constantly take the pulse of the aircraft, with flight or engine parameters flashed onto the screens if we so desired. It gave much more information on every flight, and enabled us to advise the pilot if mechanical problems were encountered.

This was now a world of complicated checklists, of glowing screens in the cockpit, duplicated in our control room in the bowels of the flight test building. If things went wrong, lights and buzzers demanded instant response. It was a world of checking that limits were not being exceeded.

Test flying was a world of disciplined flight above all else. Flight crews had detailed schedules to follow. Back-up schedules were there to be used if the primary test points could not be completed. Engineers on the ground monitored the flight and could advise if any parameter looked as if it was going out of limits. Every second of flight was used for gathering data, and every second was used to the full. To this end, flight refuelling was often used to keep the aircraft airborne as long as possible to collect even more data.

It bore very little relationship to the freedom of wheeling over the countryside in a light aircraft, turning the world upside down in a moment of exuberance in an aerobatic biplane, or thermalling over a quiet countryside in a sailplane for the last hour of precious flight before dark.

The summer of 1976 found me still flying light aircraft at weekends but yearning for something more challenging than the regular flying club aircraft. In partnership with John Scott and Barry Parkinson, I entered into a project to build a Baby Great Lakes biplane. With an 0–200 engine and only a sixteen foot wingspan, it promised to be a good little aerobatic mount. We mailed off to the USA for the plans and in due course started to build the aircraft in John's garage. The tail unit took shape first, then the welded steel tube fuselage and the wings started to come together. Each of the wings comprised a dozen or so wooden ribs, each built up from individual pieces of spruce, cut and glued in place. Each joint was reinforced with small plywood gussets. There were thousands of them. Our house was full of the aroma of glue, and drying ribs were stacked on top of cupboards and in out-of-the-way places around the house.

During the winter, our working time was drastically cut as the garage had to be laboriously heated with the aid of a pot-bellied stove which John would coax into life. The stove was invariably glowing red-hot before the temperature rose high enough for us to work on the biplane.

In my work as an aeronautical engineer I had considered it an essential part of the task to fly in as many aircraft as possible in order to broaden my experience. Having a knowledge of how the various systems worked, and how the aircraft behaved, was a vital step in turning theory into practice. This was of prime importance when dealing with the interaction of man and machine. Despite the eighty or so years since man first was successful in designing a workable flying machine, flaws still slipped past the checks in any design system, simply because of the complexity of the machines. Flight testing was the last link in a long chain, and it was there that the responsibility for the final product rested.

During Tornado design, much effort was spent in perfecting the variable-sweep wings which theoretically promised to give a smoother ride in gusty conditions at low level.

Would it work?

Once in flight test the aircraft lived up to its promise. It was gratifying to find that the advantage of variable geometry was borne out in a positive way when the Hunter flying chase on the Tornado on a low-level trip through the Lakeland hills had to pull up out of formation. Back on the ground, chase pilot Alan Love drily remarked that he thought it was time to quit when his helmet started bouncing off the canopy in the turbulence. Meanwhile the Tornado, wings swept fully back, was flying as if on rails and was completely unaffected by the gusts.

Inevitably there were smaller problems. A slight oscillation in pitch at certain flight conditions was traced to a minor flow separation around the back end of the fuselage. Various shapes were constructed in fibreglass, the fuselage recontoured with body filler, and eventually the problem was resolved after much burning of the midnight oil.

Another problem centred around the thrust reversers. Needed to give the aircraft good short-field performance, the reversers on occasion would cause directional instability on the runway when the aircraft was slowing after touching down. Saab in Sweden had the same problem on their Viggen fighter. In the case of the Tornado it was traced to an unforecast flow attachment along the vertical tail when the reverser buckets were actuated. This tended to yaw the aircraft. The reverser buckets were modified and nose-wheel steering modified before the problem was eliminated.

By 1976 the Tornado prototypes appeared at Farnborough for the first time. It was an education to see behind the scenes at a big display. For the first time I saw the brightly coloured F-15 and the YF-17 fly. These US aircraft were powerful, noisy and very agile. Impressive fighters.

Now that the Tornado flight testing was tapering off, I transferred into the Advanced Projects Department. It was a quieter, more ordered way of life than the constant alarms and excursions of a busy flight test programme. I found it more creative and just as challenging, with my job now to be constantly improving on existing aircraft and striving to beat the competition.

I had always tried to instil my enthusiasm for flying into others, whether this meant giving a beginner a quiet circuit of the local area, or a session of aerobatics at a safe height for those who wanted something different. Starting at college and later, working in the aircraft industry, I took my colleagues flying. At one stage when we were working with partner countries on international projects I would more often than not be flying the Chipmunk with one of the engineers from a partner European company safely installed in the rear cockpit. I think it helped improve aeronautical relations. It was also undeniably great fun.

Flying in England was expensive, but after the mid-seventies, with fuel costs rising, and a growing family, I found that the additional imposition of swingeing navigation charges and landing fees made cross-country flying an increasingly more expensive pastime. The final straw came when I had to fly from Blackpool back to Liverpool one day, a matter of some twenty miles, only to find that the landing charges for the trip exceeded the cost of hiring the aircraft. Trying to keep current enough to be able to fly instruments in the perennial murk of the English winter was another problem, and I eventually settled for flying only in good weather and letting my instrument rating lapse.

Tragedy struck close to home three times. Rod Turner, with whom I had flown the Chipmunk many times, spun into the ground only a few miles from Blackpool. Then Jane Murdoch was lost in an Aztec over the North Sea one winter's night. At work we lost Alan Love and Roy Bigland when their test Buccaneer crashed on the bombing range in Scotland. I had worked with them at Warton and in Germany. More good friends gone.

By this time I was back in the world of aircraft design, as a part of the team defining the next generation of aircraft to follow the Tornado. Out of the many strange shapes that emerged from Advanced Projects during this time was a delta-winged fighter with unconventional canard foreplanes, a configuration which was to reappear some years later in the EAP and EFA fighters which emerged from the Warton design office in the eighties. It was fascinating having designed these various concepts to pit the various fighters against each other on the computer, and to fly them in the simulator. Some of these fighters were tested in the wind tunnels at Warton. Although these fighters were only steps along the way, and appeared in public only as exhibition models on the British Aerospace stand at a subsequent Farnborough, they paved the way for the continuance of the Warton fighter tradition.

Things seemed fairly settled when my world was turned upside down.

Out of the blue I had an offer of a position in the aerospace industry in California. I had to decide quickly and had a few sleepless nights until I decided on my course of action. It was a very big step to make, and very much a leap in the dark. With a family to consider, and a half-built aircraft, it was not a clear-cut decision. However, I decided that the only thing to do was to sell my share in the biplane, bite the bullet . . . and set off for the New World.

10

West Coast Apprenticeship

England was shivering under half a foot of snow when I first flew out to California to take up my new job in the aerospace industry. The long hours of the non-stop flight from London provided ample opportunity to contemplate the almost legendary flying opportunities available in California. Organising my flying was certainly to be a challenge in between work and family commitments, but I looked forward to flying in year-long VFR weather. Rental costs of general aviation aircraft were only half that prevailing in the UK. In this optimistic frame of mind I was determined not to let any aeronautical opportunities pass me by.

Once into the routine of work in Los Angeles and with the family settled, I started flying at weekends. As summer approached and the daylight hours lengthened I got myself checked out on a Bellanca Citabria and started flying after work.

Clear of the Los Angeles TCA in our local practice area south of the Palos Verdes peninsula, I started renewing my rather rusty aerobatic skills. It had been a long time since I had seriously flown aerobatics but slowly I gained more confidence. As I had previously flown Chipmunks, in which the engine quit when you went inverted, the luxury of an inverted fuel system in the Citabria was new to me. Now I expanded my repertoire to include inverted flight. During my aerobatic sessions, alone in the expanse of the sky, as the sun sank I often had exhilarating views of the most spectacular Pacific sunsets. It was breathtakingly beautiful, with the sky still glowing salmon pink above me in sharp contrast with the slate-grey sea below. With dusk already falling on the city, the lights twinkling back on shore warned me to hurry home before the onset of darkness. It was all rather enjoyable.

In autumn the opportunity arose to fly a Pitts S2A, even though the hourly cost would be three times that of my Citabria. (My Californian friends raised their eyebrows at this, but from my point of view the price was only slightly more than I had been paying for the privilege of flying a Cessna 172 back in England. It didn't take long for me to make up my mind.)

So one Saturday morning I drove the eighty miles up the coast to the 'Pitts Stop' at Santa Paula. The airfield at Santa Paula was a tiny paved strip nestling between mountains and surrounded by fruit orchards. The hangars were crammed with exotic vintage aircraft, homebuilts and a variety of unusual aircraft. Owners were without exception Enthusiasts with a capital

'E'. I soon located the 'Pitts Stop' where a small but immaculate hangar housed three aircraft: a Pitts S1S; a Super Decathlon; and the Pitts S2A which I was to fly, all shoe-horned into this confined space.

I met my instructor, Dan Gray, who was to introduce me to the Pitts and we discussed how best to spend my time. The school basically offered an extensive range of aerobatic courses up to competition standard. This syllabus could be tailored to the needs of individual students. So Dan and I agreed that my time could best be split between showing me the basics of competition aerobatics and an introduction to the art of taking off and landing the Pitts. This initial session would show me what the Pitts could do . . . and for Dan to see what I could do.

After Dan had given me a thorough briefing we pushed the Pitts out of the hangar and into the sunlight. The biplane, N 31512, sported a brilliant white paint scheme coupled with eye-catching red and blue sunbursts on wings and tail surfaces. This was definitely not your average club machine and I was somewhat daunted at this stage by the prospect of actually flying this hot ship. But Dan took me through a comprehensive pre-flight; we donned parachutes, strapped in and were ready to go.

I started up and taxied out. Taxying was an art in itself with that wide white cowling blocking the view ahead and I weaved slowly out to the runway. Once I had completed the checks I lined up carefully and opened the throttle. Things certainly happened quickly on take-off in the Pitts. A blare of noise, barely time for a couple of quick stabs on the rudder pedals to keep straight and we were already airborne.

Once established in the climb I was pleasantly surprised by the stability about all three axes. This was not the twitchy machine I had been expecting. The Pitts felt a stable but very responsive machine even in my unpractised hands. Performance and control response were superb. Dan's expert coaching on this first flight left me with a healthy respect for the capabilities of the machine. Basic aerobatics were completed with much less physical effort than I had been used to, so much so that I was initially over-pulling into buffet during manoeuvres. The rate of roll given by the four ailerons was particularly impressive after the heavy-aileroned Citabria.

After an exhilarating half-hour tumbling about a cloudless sky we returned to Santa Paula and the pattern (or circuit) work. The runway at Santa Paula was both short and narrow, lined on both sides with ranks of parked aircraft. The west end of the runway was fringed by trees; the eastern end bordered by power lines. It was perhaps not the easiest field in which to master the art of landing a Pitts.

Dan coached me round on to a sideslipping final approach. So far, so good, but as I straightened out and started to flare I lost sight of the runway behind the nose. Consequently my arrival on the runway was somewhat untidy and my feet were kept busy on the pedals as we slowed. But when I finally managed to fight this spirited beast to a standstill on the runway only my pride was damaged. Subsequent landings that day were to come a little easier.

I dared even to be optimistic at the debriefing after the flight. Apart from the anticipated difficulties on landing, perhaps things had not gone too badly. But it was not to be. I sat and squirmed inwardly while Dan patiently and impartially analysed where I was going wrong in my aerobatics. Basically my aerobatics, learned Royal Air Force fashion over ten years previously, now had a distinctly 'country' flavour and I was not utilising anything like the full performance of the Pitts. If I wanted to proceed further I would have to relearn from basics, so that my loops were of the correct radius and were held circular; my aileron rolls would have a constant roll rate throughout; and my rudder technique would be refined to the required delicacy required for the Pitts.

Thoroughly humbled, I drove home.

The next weekend we tried again. I started with loops, concentrating on opening out the inverted section of the loop to a near zero g-force trajectory to give the required constant radius as the speed dropped off. We proceeded through aileron rolls (delightfully light after the Citabria) and practised Cuban eights and inverted flight before returning to base for another session of those sideslipping approaches. I felt a little happier after this flight.

As Christmas approached Dan was teaching me the finer points of hammerhead stalls and snap rolls. We explored spins of all types, including flat spins, and at the conclusion of this session we started using an alternative method for the approach into Santa Paula. Dan had me turn continuously from the end of the downwind leg as we descended. This kept the runway in sight throughout the turn and the trick was to judge the turn so that I rolled out of the turn just above the runway. I was learning.

Business kept me busy for the next few weekends and it was not until early February that I was able to return to Santa Paula. But now Dan Gray was scheduled to be pursuing his normal occupation flying an airliner at weekends and so Bill Cornick continued my education. After revision of the manoeuvres already covered, we progressed on this flight to inverted spins. I found that these were definitely an acquired taste, being extremely disorientating and uncomfortable gyrations on this first acquaintance.

I had not been particularly happy with my approaches on this occasion so the next weekend I mentioned this to Bill. Reasoning that the difficulty may have stemmed basically from fatigue after the session of aerobatics we switched the pattern work to the beginning of the sortie. But things did not improve. My difficulty now seemed to be that of assessing the point at which to flare, using only peripheral vision to pick up the white lines marking the

51

edge of the runway. The harder I tried, the worse my approaches became. I was not relaxing at all and my tenseness was really showing up on these landings.

Bill had the answer, saying that trouble of this sort was not unknown at this field with its minuscule runway, restricted approaches and the proximity of all those parked aircraft. So the next weekend we hopped across the hills to the neighbouring field at Camarillo, which sported 6,000 feet of deserted concrete. There I had a completely uneventful and enjoyable session of take-offs and landings before we cleared the pattern and headed back to our aerobatic area.

Even as we climbed the weather around us was deteriorating as a storm moved in from the Pacific. Picking our way between growing clumps of cloud under a high ceiling of stratus, we found just enough room for our purpose over the valley of the Santa Clara river. In an arena distantly walled by grey mist my progression through inverted turns went well until I tried to put it all together in a rolling circle. My efforts met with little success initially, but with a patient instructor and some perseverance we continued and I was not too displeased by the end of the session.

It was with mixed feelings that I turned the nose of the Pitts towards Santa Paula. I knew that with the weather breaking and more storms promised, my crowded schedule would not permit me to complete my planned springtime flying in the Pitts. But in these few, too short flying hours I had already come to respect and even like the Pitts. I had come to terms with the rapid take-off, touchy directional control and lack of vision on landing. After all, these idiosyncrasies were a small price to pay for the enjoyment of flying aerobatics in such a responsive machine. The Pitts was to be remembered as the most challenging and rewarding experience. I was later to fly other Pitts Specials, but these first few hours in N 31512 left a lasting impression.

11

In at the Deep End

It was sweltering hot in the front seat of the bright yellow J-3 Cub, a situation made bearable only by the gale of wind blowing through the space normally occupied by the side windows. There was a good reason for the missing windows. Under this Cub hung a pair of Edo floats, rather than the conventional wheeled landing gear. Closed windows on a floatplane would present a problem in case of an accident. So they had been removed.

However, here I was banking over the vastness of the Salton Sea in southern California. The aircraft was a 1939 vintage Cub. In this aircraft Steve Bertling was introducing me to the art of floatplane operation.

The Salton Sea had the distinction of lying some two hundred feet below sea level. On this cloudless California day the temperature was soaring towards three figures and I was sweating profusely. As I twisted round in my narrow seat, looking back over my left shoulder, I now checked my orientation relative to the spreading white V of the wake from my previous take-off.

Immediately below, the water was glassy calm. But away to the west, I could see dust devils spinning across the fields bordering this man-made lake. To the east, stretching out to the hazy horizon, white-capped waves marched across the surface of the water. We were now some twenty miles away from our base at North Shore, having flown this far to seek calmer water for my initial baptism on floats. Here in the north-western sector of the lake we had finally discovered a stretch of smoother water.

A moment ago, I had been heading downwind, but this was proving to be a day of erratic winds. As I checked, the ripples on the lake below indicated that the wind had shifted yet again. Over the clattering of the engine and the noise of the slipstream buffeting in through the open side windows, I strained to hear Steve's shouted instructions from the rear seat.

'Remember to aim for the darker water. The ripples give better depth perception.'

I nodded my assent, eased back on the throttle and we drifted round and down. Through the shimmer of the idling propeller I tried to read the water surface to ensure that we would in fact land into wind.

The Cub skimmed across the still-spreading ripples from our previous departure. There was a hiss as the floats kissed the surface, then the water grabbed at the floats and we splashed rapidly and noisily to a halt. Once at a standstill, I let the Cub weathercock into what little wind there was. This was already becoming routine. During this momentary respite I reflected how quickly I was becoming accustomed to this new aspect of flying. In fact it was only a couple of hours previously as a complete neophyte that I had started to learn the art of operating an aeroplane on floats.

My initiation had begun with the prosaic but very necessary chore of pumping dry the floats of the Cub as it bobbed at the water's edge at Salton Sea Air Service's North Shore dock, the tails of the floats resting on the edge of a wooden ramp. Once I had successfully completed this task without falling into the water, I had climbed aboard through a veritable cat's cradle of struts and bracing wires. Moving cautiously from the float, I had entered the cockpit by putting one leg over the high cockpit sill, fearful in case my sneakers should slip on the wet aluminium of the float and dump me ignominiously into the harbour in front of the onlookers. I slid into the seat and checked round the spartan cockpit. Airspeed, altitude and the odd engine instrument. A hefty rotary ignition switch. That was it. I looked around and found a cord which ran along the top of the window. The purpose of the cord was unknown.

Despite the warmth of the California day, Steve was muffled up against the anticipated draughts in the rear seat, and now padded forward to the nose of the right hand float to swing the prop. On his signal I clicked the left magneto to ON. Steve gave a deft flick of the tiny prop and the engine caught at once. The Cub started to move immediately. We puttered slowly away from the ramp and once clear of the structure Steve told me to pull the cord. I tugged on the cord.

The mystery of the cord was revealed. This lowered the water rudder mounted on the rear of the right float and gave more directional control for manoeuvring in the confines of the harbour. Steve by now had clambered into the rear seat, and once he was safely aboard I clicked the other magneto to the ON position. As the engine revs increased I taxied cautiously out into the harbour.

I was kept busy trying to absorb Steve's constant stream of instructions: watch the bow wave to judge our speed through the water; assess the effect of ailerons and rudder; keep the stick hard back and keep an eagle eye out for the weekend boaters skimming round the harbour.

We chugged out of the harbour's narrow entrance into the open water. Once clear, I closed the throttle and the Cub lost steerage way. Raising the water rudder allowed the nose to come round into the wind. As the nose steadied I opened the throttle and started the take-off run.

'Keep the stick back until I tell you,' Steve shouted. Holding the stick hard back I glanced out at the right hand float as we built up speed, waiting until the appropriate moment to get the floatplane on the step, riding on the forward part of the floats. As we accelerated the bow-wave was creeping back under the float until the fan of spray was level with my seat.

'*Now.*' The command nearly shattered my eardrums.

Easing the stick forward, I got the Cub onto the step. But nothing much happened. This was puzzling. All the books said that once a floatplane was on the step, the drag was reduced significantly as most of the float was now out of the water. We were now bouncing and rattling across the waves, but acceleration was distinctly lacking.

'Watch the nose,' Steve shouted above the din. The stick jerked forward under my hand and the nose dropped down no more than an inch on the horizon. Acceleration was immediate as the tails of the floats came clear of the water and the drag decreased. It was a graphic demonstration of the fact that the pitch attitude was absolutely critical on take-off. Maintaining an almost level attitude the Cub finally flew off the water.

During the climb it was a strange sensation to watch the altimeter wind up past zero, reminding me that the surface of the Salton Sea was almost two hundred feet below sea level. It was formed out here in the desert in 1905 when an irrigation scheme using water from the Colorado River got out of hand. In the 1950s the Douglas Skyray set the world airspeed record out here. At low level there was little traffic in this airspace, although at high altitude Navy jets still practised their air combat manoeuvring over the Salton Sea.

During the climb it was noticeable that the floats were strongly destabilising directionally. The use of rudder was mandatory during any manoeuvre, and was especially marked with any changes in power.

Once at altitude I assessed the stall behaviour of the Cub. Stalls proved to be quite normal, with marked pre-stall buffeting and a slight wing drop at the stall. Still heading out across the lake in search of calmer water, we dropped down to three hundred feet and were well out of sight of base before we found our suitable stretch of water. Steve talked me down through the first landing. We took off again and I battled with the constantly changing wind during the ensuing series of take-offs, landings and touch-and-gos.

Eventually this irritating wind stopped shifting and Steve showed me the technique for a single-float take-off, a trick to help the floatplane unstick from glassy water. This seemed a little like a circus trick, but was very effective in breaking the suction on the float. During the take-off, as the ailerons became effective, Steve showed me how to heave the stick over and lift one float off the water, stopping the bank before it became excessive and the wingtip got too near the water.

Circling take-offs came next. This was a proven technique for getting airborne from a confined stretch of water. It seemed inappropriate to be doing this while the nearest land to us was a blur on the horizon. But further north in the western US they fly anything and everything on floats. I was later to fly into Vancouver and watch Otters, Beavers and a horde of Cessnas all operating happily out of Vancouver Harbour. Anecdotes abound where floatplanes operate. Getting a heavily laden Beech 18 off the surface of a small lake in Canada needed all the expertise a pilot could muster. I met some Alaskan bush pilots. More stories. They were all expert pilots, but all started on Cubs or Cessnas.

We flew hither and thither in our search for sheltered water as the wind shifted erratically. We tried flying in the lee of the lakeside. But this day even the shoreline was ill-defined, with stretches of marsh, trees and even power poles punctuating the surface some hundreds of yards from the shoreline. After a succession of torrential winter storms, the Salton Sea was well above its normal level. Roads ended abruptly at the water's edge; houses had been inundated. Even the airstrip back at North Shore was unusable, with half of the runway under water.

So I took off with the tops of telegraph poles marking my horizon, or roared along with clumps of grass sliding past the wingtip while ducks skittered away from the floats.

We had been out nearly two hours and the rod of the fuel gauge was dropping down into the filler cap on the cowling in front of me. To finish off our session, Steve taught me the art of glassy-water landings. On flat-calm days it was impossible for the pilot to judge his height above the water. More than one floatplane had been lost by flying into the water prematurely. The trick was to keep a gentle and constant rate of descent while maintaining a precise approach airspeed. So now I learned to hold that attitude exactly and keep things stabilised until the floats touched ever so gently and we found ourselves on the water.

Our fuel was getting low and it was time to point the nose of the Cub towards North Shore. It was a picturesque return which would have gladdened the heart of any Audubon fan as we threaded our way between skeins of geese overhead and pelicans flapping across the surface below. Landing in the lee of the North Shore breakwater, I taxied carefully back into the harbour.

The next bit was tricky. I had to point the Cub at the sloping wooden ramp and take it ashore with a burst of power. Despite Steve's assurances I could visualise the Cub doing a ski-jump off the ramp and ending up in the office building just behind. But we were not there yet. Judging the drift on the water was difficult enough. Following Steve's directions I leaned out of the cabin and lined up the right hand float with the ramp. As the Cub drifted closer, I pulled on the cord to raise the water rudder then, before the nose could drift off-line, I said a quick prayer and shoved the throttle fully forward. Amid a blare of noise the Cub blasted out of the water and slid up the ramp to a nose-high stop, clear of the water. I breathed a sigh of relief and climbed shakily out of the cockpit.

That was the end of flying for the day.

The Cub was refuelled from a tank in the back of a pick-up truck, hosed down thoroughly to remove all traces of salt water, then lashed securely to the ramp to guard against overnight squalls.

As an orange sun dropped westwards through the tops of the gently rustling palms, I realised that this day had been more than simply a transition to another aircraft. Other pilots had told me that flying a seaplane was a unique experience. So it was proving to be.

Without the constant pressure of flying in the high-density traffic system of the LA Basin, I was finding that seaplane flying was an undertaking which demanded a genuine mindshaft, reflecting a more leisurely outlook on life, in a way more akin to boating.

At eight o'clock the next morning we were already flying our little yellow machine. In the centre of the lake I drifted down to a gentle landing on the glassy water. Once the floats had stopped cutting their wakes through the water I killed the engine. So there we were, miles from land, sitting in the centre of a spreading circle of ripples. But we were there for a purpose. Steve had chosen this setting to have me practise sailing backwards towards an imaginary dock, using only the effects of the breeze against deflected ailerons and rudder to determine our direction of movement. Once I had mastered the technique in unobstructed waters, we could go and try it with a real dock.

That was the intention, but by now the breeze had dropped to a flat calm. So we sat and talked while the sun blazed down. Our voices were lost in the silence pressing down on this vast expanse of water. Every so often a cat's paw of wind would set the Cub rocking uneasily, and the silence was broken by the soft gurgling of water under the floats.

Eventually the breeze returned. Leaning out and looking past the tail, working stick and rudder hard to make the ailerons and rudder flop out into the fitful breeze, I made the Cub slowly tack to left and right across the surface of the lake as I aimed for this imaginary dock. Eventually Steve nodded his approval. It was time to put into practice the techniques I had learned so far.

Firing up the engine I took off, flying south-west to the shoreline, then following the coast south until we were overhead Salton City. This grandiose title belonged to a scattered collection of houses lost in an immensity of parched desert. As I circled, Steve pointed out a short stretch of canal leading from the south side of town and ending in the Salton Sea. This was to be our landing site.

I turned on to finals for the canal. Something seemed wrong. Then I realised that out here over the desert I was very aware of the floats underneath us. A week ago I was uncomfortable flying over water. How my perceptions were changing. This uncomfortable feeling persisted until we were over the water again. The canal seemed terribly narrow after all those landings on the vastness of the lake. It felt like threading the eye of the needle on approach, but there was ample room between the banks and our wingtips and the landing itself went off perfectly.

As the water in the canal was glass-smooth, take-off was going to require the use of a little bit of expertise to get us airborne. So a single-float take-off was not just an academic exercise. Once I opened the throttle and the Cub was moving briskly through the water I rocked the Cub onto the left float with aileron, using rudder to keep straight as we skimmed past fishermen and children playing at the water's edge. As advertised, we broke cleanly from the water and went zipping along the canal.

This was proving to be fun.

I got a few more canal landings under my belt before flying a few miles further down the coast. Here a sandy beach bordering a sinuous inlet was the site where Steve wanted me to practise beaching the Cub.

We landed and I gently drove the Cub ashore until the nose of one float was just on the edge of the beach. As I swung out of the cockpit, Steve enlivened the moment by warning me not to forget to hang on to the mooring rope. He drily assured me that this latter occurrence was not unknown as the pilot's attention was invariably concentrated on jumping from float to beach without falling in. This inevitably resulted in a dramatic situation with the pilot left on the beach and the floatplane drifting inexorably away from land . . .

I eventually managed to accomplish this single-handed operation successfully, thankful that I had actually managed to beach and moor the Cub without running us aground, falling in or letting the Cub drift away.

After passing the time of day with the locals who had magically materialised out of the desert to watch the fun, we climbed aboard to return to North Shore. Taking off from the inlet in a flat calm was a good time for me to put that curving take-off technique into practice. Sure enough we were well round the bend of the inlet before the floats could be persuaded to leave the water. Eventually we unstuck, climbed to an awe-inspiring height of fifty feet and bored across the twenty miles or so of Salton Sea which separated us from North Shore.

Back at base we refuelled both Cub and crew. After lunch I had to take my test for the FAA rating. Brad Bertling, the other half of Salton Sea Air Service, was my examiner and he occupied the rear seat while I took the Cub out of the harbour. Once outside the breakwater, I found that the wind had risen since my morning flight and the use of rough-water techniques was for real. Take-off seemed to take an eternity as the Cub's floats butted into the waves. As the floats hit each wave with a teeth-jarring thump, sheets of spray flew in all directions. It was a relief to get airborne, and we quickly found a slightly more sheltered patch of water to demonstrate to Brad that I was capable of operating an aircraft in this new environment. All went well and it seemed only a few minutes before I was bringing the Cub back into the harbour for the last time, confidently running the Cub up the ramp and killing the ignition as it slid to a halt.

Brad signed me off for the rating in the tiny office. All that remained was for Steve and Brad to wish me well with my flying. Both Brad and Steve had previously taught flying in the crowded skies over the LA Basin, but had decided to set up business out here, preferring the solitude of the desert way of life to the bustle of urban living.

As I set off for the long drive back to the urban sprawl of Los Angeles, I mused that as a way of life it had certain advantages. There was undeniably a magic about floatplane flying.

12

The Reason Why

Coming to the USA was a breath of fresh air after the problems of private flying that to me had assumed an overwhelming importance in England by the seventies. Operating costs of aircraft were much less in the USA, principally because of the cheapness of the fuel. On top of this the FAA gave lots of freedom to the individual pilot and landing fees were largely non-existent. Added to this, weather was generally more favourable – in California at any rate.

As I got back into flying, I started adding various ratings to my licence in order to increase my experience. My multi-engined licence was obtained on a Piper Apache, one of the earliest on the US register. I found it an honest aeroplane, although this particular example could be cranky on occasion by having a left hand engine which could not be persuaded to restart in flight. Basically it handled like a big Cub and I occasionally landed the Apache on the short runway at Torrance without fuss.

Next came the instrument rating, and I criss-crossed the Los Angeles Basin night after night wearing a hood to blank out the sight of the brightly lit fairyland of lights. Occasionally we flew in clouds and rain. Doing it for real. Gradually the complicated clearances, to reporting points in the ocean with quirky names like LIMBO, PERCH and ALBAS became as familiar as street names to a commuter. Approaches to the commercial airports at San Diego or Long Beach would be enlivened by the knowledge that an airliner was following me down the approach.

My commercial training was taken in a 172 RG, almost the same familiar Cessna in which I had spent so many hours, but now with the complexity of a retractable gear.

Flying in California had its own set of operational problems as well. High temperatures in the summer led to frequent battles with engine cooling and I found that oil temperatures often pegged on the upper limit during climb. High density altitudes were common during the summer months and flying a low-powered aircraft out of a small field with the temperature over a hundred degrees Fahrenheit gave an appreciation of the performance figures in the manual.

Extensive forest fires were common in southern California. When combined with the often present inversion over the LA Basin, this could lead to a situation where visibility was drastically reduced by layers of smoke. One day in particular the LA Basin seemed ringed by fire as half a dozen large fires burned in the hills. As I climbed into the inversion flying a Citabria the smell of burning timber became strong. The air temperature rose twenty or thirty degrees, sending scorching blasts of smoke-laden air into the cabin through the fresh-air vents. It was an uncomfortable few minutes until I climbed through the inversion into cooler air.

A further hazard was the Santa Ana wind. This was an offshore wind which blew out of the surrounding mountains when a high pressure area formed inland in the winter months. Below the canyons, a Venturi effect magnified the effects of the wind and it was not unusual for extensive gale damage to result. Aircraft were ill-suited to resist such a wind storm. Hangars were occasionally blown down, with aircraft ripped from their tie-down ropes and flung carelessly across the ramp. For aircraft in flight the Santa Ana wind caused problems ranging from severe turbulence to having to cope with high and erratic winds on landing. All this usually took place under an innocuous blue sky. If a Santa Ana condition was forecast it was normally a day to leave the aircraft on the ground.

Aviation traffic in southern California was heavy. I flew out of Torrance, Orange County and Long Beach, airports which ranked high in the number of aircraft movements per year in the USA. Generally speaking the controllers managed to integrate the general aviation and airline traffic satisfactorily. However in bad weather often there could be quite a delay on the ground before you could be slotted into the system. Occasionally the only solution was to shut down until your allotted time slot arrived.

In the USA general aviation was much more necessary than in England. After all, Los Angeles still lay at the edge of the desert. Highways crossed the desert, but the average day's drive could be five or six hundred miles. The US system, with access to the airways system available even to the VFR pilot, proved well suited to the transportation of people over long distances by air.

I could not help reflecting on the differences in flying in the USA and Europe while climbing out over Long Beach early one morning. The sky just after dawn was that translucent green found only on clear days as the sun rises. Looking through the arc of the Apache's port propeller I watched Mount Baldy silhouetted against the growing light to the east. Visibility on this winter morning was unlimited and the range of the San Gabriel mountains stretched eastward for a hundred miles in snow-capped majesty. It was a privilege and a pleasure to be flying on such a morning. The only discordant note was a slight mismatch in the engine speeds, causing an unpleasant beat in the engine noise. I fiddled with the pitch levers and succeeded in synchronising the engines. As the engines settled into a smooth roar, I levelled off over the Seal Beach VOR and trimmed for level flight. Looking out over the nose towards the Cajon Pass to the east, I could already see the vapour trails of the Phantoms flying out of George AFB, which lay a hundred miles or so to the east.

Even at our relatively modest 140 knots, Las Vegas lay less than three hours away across the burning desert, halving the time to make that interminable trip by road as I had done so many times before. The beauty of the system here was that the FAA operated largely for the benefit of all users. Airliners, general aviation aircraft and commuter airliners all used the airways here, in VFR or IFR conditions. From my point of view it made my life simpler. The various controlling facilities would monitor my journey across the state boundary as far as Nevada. All this was largely free, in contrast to the growing tide of navigation charges which had tried to strangle general aviation in Europe.

Basically the sky was a world in which I generally flew alone, but on occasion I could share it with friends or family, watching the beauty of a sunset, or sunlight playing along the coastline. Springtime was an especially pretty season when flying in California, as large areas of the coastline were rimmed with purple as patches of ice-plant started to blossom, while further inland the California poppies turned the desert in the Antelope Valley into a riotous stretch of red and orange blooms. The sight of the Los Angeles Basin at night, with millions of lights stretching for miles in every direction, made a spectacular sight. At night the freeways were turned into rivers of red lava and white light. Airport beacons flashed green and white and the sky was full of winking strobes and anti-collision beacons. It could be a crowded sky.

This same sky could also give rise to some strange sights. Did I believe in UFOs? Well, before coming to California I was not convinced either way. However, keeping an open mind was one thing; actually seeing something rather strange was a different matter . . .

One moonless night at Camarillo airport I was intent on copying down my instrument clearance for my return flight to Torrance, having switched the radio to a ground channel to do so. My engine was running, so I was oblivious of any external noise, when something made me look up, some sense of not being alone.

A hundred yards away, directly in front of my idling propeller, hanging motionless thirty feet above the twin blue lines of lights marking the taxi-way, was a weird Christmas tree of pulsating lights set against the dark mass of the hills. Red and white lights flashed and shimmied in the gloom, while strange flashes of red were spun off intermittently into the blackness.

For the first time in my life, I started to feel the hair stand up on the back of my neck. What on earth was I looking at?

Transfixed, I stared at this apparition, which bore no resemblance to anything I had seen before. At that moment I would not have been surprised if little green men had descended from it.

Then the radio crackled into life: '52 Echo, be aware of an Army helicopter coming past you. We are letting him air-taxi down the taxiway to the ramp'. Reason returned. I started breathing again. As this strange beast hesitantly crept nearer, the strange lights proved to be the effects of the anti-collision beacons reflecting off the twin tandem rotors of this dark-painted Chinook. In the slight wind the Chinoock was crabbed slightly so that its green position lights were hidden from me, with the red position lights and its landing lights giving this strange effect to a commonplace occurrence . . .

A casual approach to flying usually has tragic consequences. Occasionally the odds can be beaten, either by skill or by some favourable intervention from the gods.

One day at Hawthorne I was at the end of the runway when an unfamiliar Cessna appeared on final approach. It was against the morning sun and my attention was attracted to it as it drew nearer by the fact that the silhouette was somewhat different from the normal Cessna 172s. I looked again. As the Cessna came over the fence, I could see that trailing from the rear of the aircraft was a large concrete block on a four-foot length of rope. In the USA any aircraft not hangared is tied down overnight. Wings and tail are tied down to these fifty-pound blocks. Normally this is sufficient to tether the aircraft against any gusts of wind. On this occasion the pilot had obviously neglected to remove the block prior to flight.

However, he had managed to taxi the length of the field dragging the block with him, then succeeded in taking off despite now having a centre of gravity somewhat further aft than normal. After a quick circuit of the field with the control wheel pushed firmly forward to stay straight and level he was returning to rectify the situation when I saw him.

The Cessna touched down normally, with the block simultaneously hitting the concrete and exploding into fragments. Turning off at the next intersection he taxied back to his tiedown area, dejectedly dragging the rope behind him. A hard way for him to learn a lesson.

Nobody laughed. He was still alive. The controller closed the runway for thirty minutes while the maintenance crew swept the debris from the runway.

I found that working in the aerospace industry in California was quite different from the ordered way of life in England. It was a dynamic environment in which jobs could evaporate almost overnight with budget cuts. Even for high-level positions, job security was defined as being employed until the end of the week. Once bitten, as the saying goes, so I added a second string to my bow by branching out on my own as a freelance writer. My previous writing, and my jet-flying background, provided opportunities to fly in a number of fairly exotic aircraft, including military jets.

Jet flying in particular had a magical quality. At 30,000 feet over the western United States, a good portion of California's Central valley lay beneath, with the State visible from the Channel Islands behind the trailing edge of the swept wing while San Francisco Bay lay ahead of the nose. The mountain ranges had an almost lunar quality to them, with no sign of habitation from this altitude. The sheer size of the United States never failed to awe me, after flying for many years in England where it was possible to see right across the country, from the North Sea to the Irish Sea on a clear day.

On occasion cruising at altitude over cloud I could look down at our contrail racing over the blinding cloud deck below. At the head of the contrail was the shadow of the speeding aircraft. Surrounding the shadow was a perfect rainbow, a multi-coloured halo, seen only by aviators and mountain climbers. Explainable completely by the laws of physics, it was nevertheless still a beautiful sight.

At altitude, a significant proportion of earth's fragile atmosphere lay below. Breathing through an oxygen mask was sufficient to remind me that the environment at this height was hostile to man and only technology enabled man to exist up here for any length of time. In return, seeing the sun redden through veils of smoke from forest fires or watching steam ooze from the blasted stump of Mount St Helens was a reminder of the fragile hold we had on the surface of this planet, and overall we were still subservient to the powers of nature.

13

Test Pilot for a Day

A scorching wind from the high desert of southern California moaned around the needle nose of an F-104 Starfighter, permanently earth-bound but pointing skyward on a pylon outside the low building housing the USAF Test Pilot's School at Edwards Air Force Base. A rocket engine mounted at the base of the vertical tail showed that this was one of those NF-104s which explored the edge of the atmosphere twenty years ago.

Of the three original NF-104s with their 6,000lb LR-121 rocket engines and reaction controls, one of the three survived a mid-air explosion of the rocket motor and made it back to Edwards and the sanctuary of Rogers Dry Lake, landing with tail feathers in shreds. Another was lost when Chuck Yeager, as Commandant of the Test Pilot School, entered a flat spin during a ballistic trajectory flight at over 100,000 feet. He rode the bird down to fourteen thousand feet before baling out, only to be severely burned by the rocket of the ejection seat.

In those days, and for the previous twenty years, Edwards was the fabled home of the test pilots, later to be immortalised in Tom Wolfe's book *The Right Stuff*. A breed who would fly anything, anywhere.

In the eighties, had things changed?

Test flying even in the time I had been involved with it in England was becoming more of a science than an art. As aircraft became more sophisticated, test flying was increasingly concerned with systems testing, not just the handling qualities of the aircraft. However, at the USAF Test Pilot School the classical techniques of performance and flying qualities were still taught in addition to systems testing. The performance phase included aerodynamics and test techniques, while students were taught the skills required to evaluate all aspects of aircraft performance. One unique part of this course was the low lift/drag flying applicable to lifting body or shuttle operations. (Most of the astronauts were alumni of this exclusive school.)

During the flying qualities part of the intensive 46-week course the students learned to evaluate the handling of a range of aircraft in the school's fleet. Resident aircraft ranged from the F-4 to A-37, from Beaver to KC-135, together with a variable stability Learjet and a T-33 to demonstrate both the problems and the solutions encountered when assessing handling qualities. The students and staff assured me that it was the best job in the air force.

What was it like, learning to be a test pilot? I was given the opportunity to find out when I was invited to fly with the USAF Test Pilot School.

Our mount for this mission was the supersonic Northrop T-38, nicknamed the White Rocket during its long career with the USAF and NASA. I flew with Colonel Mel Hayashi, Commandant of the Test Pilot School, for a mission which would cover a sample of the teaching techniques used during the handling and performance portions of the course.

In addition to the handling points on our flight, we briefed for a simulated shuttle approach which would culminate in a lakebed landing. This was treated routinely as just another segment of the course dealing with low L/D flying. As Colonel Hayashi explained, we would simply aim for a triangular marker painted on the lakebed, then switch to another marker as we flared. From my point of view a 280 knots power-off descent with flaps, airbrake and gear down promised to be interesting. I had watched the NASA Gulfstream apparently dive-bombing the lakebed doing precisely this manoeuvre when the astronauts were training for their shuttle landings. It was terrifying to watch. I started to wonder why I had volunteered.

Before we walked out to the aircraft Colonel Hayashi gave me a comprehensive briefing on emergency procedures in the T-38, bale-out procedures and the actions required if we should have a bird strike. We were due to fly at two o'clock in the afternoon and I had spent most of the morning being fitted with flight suit, boots, helmet and oxygen mask. Last of all came the g-suit. A tight fit was essential for it to do its job correctly, and I was carefully hooked, laced and zipped into the g-suit.

It was eighty degrees Fahrenheit and a hot dry wind was sweeping across the acres of concrete of the Edwards ramp as we walked out to the white stiletto of our T-38. It was a long walk out across the ramp, helmet in hand, with the buckles on my back-type parachute clinking and the bulky g-suit making it awkward to walk. The tower was giving the visibility as eighty-five miles and the snow-capped San Gabriel mountains to the south shimmered incongruously in the distance as we approached the T-38. It was a small aircraft, but looked wickedly fast just sitting on the ramp.

I climbed the rear ladder and parked my helmet on the far cockpit sill, tucking my gloves and kneepad up onto the coaming of the rear blast screen. I swung the parachute into the rear seat, hooked up the survival pack connectors and then climbed in. Our crew chief helped me connect up the parachute harness, g-suit and the seat straps while Colonel Hayashi pre-flighted the aircraft and then climbed into the front cockpit.

Isolated in the rear cockpit, I donned helmet, mask and gloves. Plugging in the various connections I was reassured by the doll's eye oxygen indicator blinking down by my right knee as I breathed in and out. As the intercom came alive we established communications.

66

Test Pilot for a Day

As Colonel Hayashi hit the starter button the right hand J-85 started to motor over. At fourteen per cent rpm the engine lit with a rumble, sending the turbine temperature needle scurrying round the dial. The engine wound up to idle power, whining away behind me while the left hand engine was started. With both engines running, the flight controls were checked for full and free movement. Forewarned, I made sure my knees were out of the way of the stick. By now our crew chief had stationed himself in front of the T-38 and pantomimed the control surface movements as the stick was moved. Here, way in front of the wings, it was difficult to see the control surfaces, even in my rear view mirrors on the canopy arch.

The controls checked out OK. All that remained was to pull out the safety pins for the canopy jettison and the ejection seat, hold them up for the crew chief to see, then stow them away. Our callsign was COBRA 01, the number reserved for the School Commandant, and the tower cleared us to taxi for the active runway. A burst of power persuaded COBRA 01 into motion and we taxied down the ramp, the open canopies nodding as we rumbled over the joints in the concrete.

The Edwards ramp was crowded with the resident F-4s and F-111s. We rolled out across the field, stopping at the marshalling point near the end of the runway. Here two crewmen made a final visual inspection of each aircraft, checking for leaks or discrepancies. For safety's sake our gloved hands were kept in full view, away from any switches. I rested my hands on my canopy arch, well clear of the controls while the crew scurried about under the aircraft. Satisfied, they ran clear and waved us back to the taxi-way.

It was time to button up and I reached up and manually lowered the canopy, pushing the locking lever forward on the right hand wall until it clunked home and the canopy warning light extinguished. My head was almost touching the canopy and I blipped the electric seat adjustment down until I could get some clearance between my helmet and the canopy.

We rolled gently out onto runway 04, checking that there was no one on finals, and lined up precisely on the centreline that stretched out to the shimmering lakebed in the distance. Mindful of the warning about bird strikes I lowered my smoked visor as COBRA 01 was cleared for take-off.

As the power levers advanced to the military power detent and the brakes were released, we started to move. The T-38 accelerated rapidly, keeping straight initially with differential braking, then the power levers went fully forward to maximum power and the nozzles opened as the afterburners lit. The right hand nozzle was fractionally slow, but once both were lit the acceleration continued to increase inexorably. At 155 knots the T-38 flew off the ground and started to accelerate rapidly once the gear and doors were tucked away. As the ground dropped away we came out of afterburner and the acceleration decreased perceptibly.

I set up the climb as briefed at 350 knots, still at military power. My task was made easier by the special instrumentation fitted in the School's T-38s. In these aircraft the standard ASI and altimeter had been replaced by single-pointer instruments. As the ASI was graduated in knots, with one complete revolution reading one hundred knots, airspeed could be read to an accuracy of one to two knots. Initially I found that I could not match that accuracy and we pursued a slightly roller-coaster path as I got used to the power controls of the T-38. It was a bit lighter than the Cessna 172 RG I had been flying the week before. We settled into the climb at 4,000 ft/min and some three minutes later I levelled out at 15,000 feet.

Visibility was spectacular from the T-38. The rear seat was set some ten inches higher than the front seat and I could see straight ahead over the forward ejection seat. Apart from the canopy frames and the glass blast screen between the cockpits I had an unobstructed view out of the canopy ahead and to either side. By craning around I could just see the wings following us. It was easier to look in the rear view mirrors on my canopy arch to check behind.

Colonel Hayashi pointed out the landmarks in the local area while we positioned for our first test point. We were heading towards Owens Dry Lake some 60 miles to the north, with the white-capped saw-toothed bulk of the Sierra Nevada range of mountains stretching off our left side and extending for perhaps a hundred miles. The highest, Mount Whitney, 14,494 feet, was clearly visible on our horizon. Below us stretched the dusty sagebrush wastes of the Mojave desert. Volcanic plugs dotted the plain below and although it was a completely alien landscape I realised with a sense of déjà vu that of course I did know this scene. While I had been growing up it had been the backdrop for all that spectacular footage of test flying from the X-1, Skyrocket and X-15 projects. These were hallowed skies for anyone involved in any way with test flying. It was a strange sensation.

Colonel Hayashi started by showing me how a student was taught to set up a typical stable test point. No screaming dives to the edge of the envelope on this flight. The essence of test flying was accuracy. The limits for me to fly to were plus or minus two knots and we were aiming to establish a data point at exactly 15,000 feet and 300 knots.

In a strange aircraft, the test pilot first had to estimate the power to set up the first point, so we chose a deliberately low power setting to start. At exactly 15,000 feet the power was inched up to eighty-seven per cent on the J85s; stick forces were trimmed out on the coolie hat trim switch on the top of the hefty stick grip and we waited for the aircraft to stabilise. It settled at 295 knots, so rpm was inched up to eighty-nine per cent.

This gained us two knots and so the power was increased in tiny increments and the process repeated until at ninety-one per cent we had exactly 300 knots. At this point our hands were taken off the controls to see if we were trimmed out. The T-38 hummed along, rock-steady. It seemed easy enough.

Now it was my turn. My task was to set up a point at 240 knots. With throttles back to idle we slowed to about 220 knots and I started inching the power up. In my unpractised hands the exercise proved to be a slightly more lengthy procedure than I had anticipated. By the time I had the situation more or less under control and had trimmed out the stick forces, we were within five miles of the eastern boundary of our Restricted Military Airspace and the controller wanted us to turn back west. I began to appreciate why the minimum requirements for entry to the Test Pilot School included a thousand hours of jet time. Flying to this accuracy had to be second nature before embarking on a venture like this.

Next on our flight card was an acceleration from 250 knots to M 0.9 while maintaining exactly 15,000 feet. At M 0.9 we would bring back the power to idle and decelerate under a constant 3g until we hit the aerodynamic limit which would be marked by heavy airframe buffeting.

As we accelerated I was aware that the tiniest corrections in pitch were constantly required to maintain us at constant altitude as the speed increased. As the angle of attack decreased I could see the nose inching lower against the horizon. Above M 0.85 a small-amplitude directional snaking appeared. This was a transient effect of the yaw damper system.

At M 0.9 as the power levers were brought back to idle we flipped into a steep left hand bank. As the needle of the accelerometer locked on to 3g my g-suit inflated, pressing against my legs and abdomen to restrict the flow of blood away from my head. The turn tightened and the speed drastically reduced as the induced drag increased.

It was noticeably difficult to breathe as I strained against the g-force and tried to write notes on my kneepad. Below three hundred knots the ride started to get louder and rougher as the airflow started breaking away behind the canopy and over the wings. At 250 knots the T-38 was protesting by giving us a very uncomfortable ride. The stick went forward to unload the g-force and the T-38 came back into level flight.

Now it was my turn to try this. Bringing the power levers back up to military power, I watched the gauges all start winding up. Flying this accurately took me back to the days when I was sweating through my instrument rating. It was just as challenging. I found that by concentrating hard on the altimeter I could maintain altitude precisely at 15,000 feet, although as the Machmeter crept past M 0.8 it was becoming increasingly difficult to maintain altitude exactly.

At M 0.9 I brought the power levers back to the idle stop and attempted to set up the required 3g deceleration in the turn. In an all but vertical bank my attention was divided between keeping the altimeter at 15,000 feet and maintaining the correct bank angle. I found this task easier said than done. There were few cues for speed and attitude outside the cockpit and while I was trying to keep the horizon in the right place I found that the g-force backed off and the g-suit deflated. My eye finally caught the movement of the needle and I pulled back until we hit 3g.

We hit the buffet at around 280 knots and it got progressively worse until I could feel the aircraft starting to wallow round in the heavy airframe buffeting. That was enough of a limit for me. Pushing the stick forward to unload the gs I powered us back into level flight to set up for the next point on the text card, a constant airspeed descent at 300 knots. After a suggestion from the front cockpit that I try eighty per cent rpm for this, I was on my own. I pulled the throttles back, checked that the speedbrake was out and we started sliding down the sky. It was difficult initially for me to keep the speed constant; I was still tending to overcontrol. In jets small changes in speed generate large variations in the rate of descent.

We levelled at 10,000 feet to demonstrate the effects of flying on the back of the drag curve. The T-38, designed by Northrop in the fifties to introduce pilots to the Century Series supersonic fighters, had all the characteristics of the early supersonic jets, with a low aspect ratio wing giving high induced drag at high angles of attack. The slower you flew, the more power was needed to combat the drag.

Flight behaviour in this region had its own characteristics. Our demonstration point was 190 knots and 10,000 feet, with gear down and flaps at sixty per cent. I tried to remember the classroom briefing. In this regime altitude was maintained with power while speed was now controlled by pitch, reversing our previous technique at the higher speeds.

For our budding student test pilot, accuracy was the goal, as it was at the higher speed. The technique was to bring the power up in increments until 94 per cent on each engine kept the altimeter locked on to 10,000 feet; meanwhile the speed was maintained at exactly 190 knots by tiny fore-and-aft corrections on the stick. At this speed we were getting into an area of small amplitude wing rock.

At this point I took control of the aircraft again to set up my point at 180 knots and 10,000 feet. I met with indifferent success initially, finding that the power required just to stop us descending had the throttles almost up towards military power. It was fast becoming a juggling act as my changes in pitch to keep the speed constant were in turn magnified by instrument lags, and the fact that I was not letting things settle out. Gradually the situation was sorted out and we settled at the required 180 knots, nose way up in the air and engines almost all the way up to 100 per cent as the engine thrust fought the induced drag from the tiny wing. This was the purpose of the exercise and I was learning fast.

At the eastern limit of our airspace again we turned west, pausing while an F-16 flashed past some 2,000 feet above on a reciprocal course. Edwards airspace was very congested. Civil aircraft were warned to keep well away. With a dozen or so military jets airborne on various tests at any one time, maintaining separation was a full-time task for the controllers.

My next task was to find the g-force level at 300 knots at which the T-38 could just maintain sustained flight at military power. This would give a checkpoint on the specific excess energy curve of the aircraft. Combat aircraft live or die on specific excess energy in combat. Aircraft designers need to know how their aircraft measure up to their calculations by checking on specific excess energy.

I set up a level turn at military power and gradually increased the bank angle, pulling back to keep the g-force increasing and maintaining the speed on exactly 300 knots. We could just maintain 2.4g at this flight condition, with thrust just equal to drag at this point. Easing the stick back gave fractionally more g-force and sure enough the speed started to drop. This checked out with the book figure.

Colonel Hayashi gave me a break from this hard work and we took five minutes out to fly the T-38 through some aerobatics. Barrel rolls were especially fun, using the distant snow-capped peak of Mt Whitney as a reference point. I found the T-38 a delightful aircraft to manoeuvre but typical of any fast jet it certainly used a lot of sky as we effortlessly soared and rolled between 8,000 feet and 15,000 feet. Aerobatics were exhilarating and roll rate was spectacularly fast, as good as a Pitts Special.

Watching the fuel gauges, we could see that it was time to head back to Edwards. However, we found that Murphy strikes in flight test scheduling just as much as in other types of aviation. By now the wind had strengthened from the east and the traffic pattern in use now cut right across the airspace over the lakebed.

We needed that airspace to complete our scheduled Shuttle-type approach and lakebed landing. Peering over the side I could see the aiming markers sharply contrasted against the white lakebed, but regretfully we had to pass that item by.

As a precaution, before flight we had indeed briefed a couple of alternate test points, and now we started to descend towards the lakebed for a practice tower fly-by. This was a pure flight test exercise in which the student had to set up a precise flight condition. Another of those tests requiring the utmost accuracy. The exact flight parameters had to be maintained while flying past an observer in a special fly-by tower on the lakebed. By sighting on the aircraft the observer could establish the altitude exactly. Later comparison of the aircraft's known position with the instrument readings enabled a check to be made of the pitot and static pressure errors in the aircraft system.

71

The cockpit was very quiet as we descended. The tower gave us updated pressure readings for the altimeter which I set in on my panel. COBRA 01 was now cleared for a tower fly-by. As the throttles went forward we accelerated to our briefed speed of 400 knots as the airfield slid past on our right hand side, with the gleaming white surface of Rogers Dry Lake beyond the base.

Down now to 200 feet over the ground the airspeed stabilised at 400 knots and the power levers were left alone from this point on. We banked hard right over the eastern portion of the lakebed, aiming for a stubby pylon which marked the beginning of the tower fly-by run. From the base of the pylon a black line arrowed off across the lakebed into the distance.

I strained against the g-force as the pylon flashed past less than a hundred feet below and we flicked back into level flight, seemingly balanced over this black line while the lakebed streamed past to either side. This time of day would not be a good one for taking data, Colonel Hayashi remarked conversationally, as the turbulence over the lakebed was causing the airspeed to fluctuate two or three knots either side of our datum, enough to invalidate the data. For serious results, these tests were invariably carried out in the early morning, before the sun had heated the desert.

We streaked past the tower and on across the airfield.

Continuing on at low altitude, Colonel Hayashi showed me what performance of the T-38 was like at low level. Throttles went forward and accelerating in military power the speed was now up to 500 knots. It was an exhilarating ride at this low level. Out of the corner of my eye I could see our shadow flicking across the sagebrush-covered desert. We were heading north and as the terrain got rougher the jolting ride became worse in the turbulence. Even at this speed the cockpit was still quiet. I was writing more notes when we ran into a patch of rough air and I was slammed against my straps, with the airspeed fluctuating violently.

Enough of that. The quickest way out of the turbulence was upwards and we pulled up at 5g. This was definitely enough to stop me taking notes. We arrowed up to 10,000 feet, coasting inverted over the top of a giant loop and rolling upright in an Immelmann manoeuvre to head back to base for some pattern work.

Descending to the traffic pattern altitude, we ran in over the field. Fuel was down to 1,100lb as we broke to the right at 300 knots some 1,500 feet above the field. Power levers were pulled back and as the T-38 decelerated through 240 knots, gear and flaps came down. It all happened very quickly. Speed was down to 175 knots on a tightly curving base leg, tapering off to 155 knots on finals. Remembering the behaviour of the T-38 at low speed I was not surprised to find that the power was way up just to keep us flying with the high drag from gear and flaps added to the induced drag from that vestigial wing. The angle of attack indicator on my coaming was in the green. Over the overrun we went to military power, cleaned up and overshot. We were now at 1,000lb of fuel. The J85 jets were thirsty at low altitude and the gauges were dropping rapidly.

Another T-38 and an F-16 joined us in the pattern and we decided to make the next landing a full stop. With fuel down to 900lb, this time we banked round on our curving approach with three greens, flaps full down and airspeed at 155 knots. We touched down on the numbers, then whistled along the runway, nose kept high for aerodynamic braking until the speed dropped to one hundred knots. The nose was allowed to drop, then gentle braking brought the speed down to a reasonable pace and we turned off the runway.

We cracked the canopies open to taxi back. The desert air was dry and pleasantly cool. At the end of the taxi-way we waited while an all-white A-7 taxied past, part of the never-ending pattern of flying at Edwards. Colonel Hayashi wheeled the T-38 back into our parking slot. I inserted the seat pins as the J85s whistled down into silence.

This flight had given me an insight into the challenging world of teaching pilots to be test pilots. I had found out the hard way that there is a world of difference in some respects between theory and practice. Classroom work is not enough. Flying the T-38 and the other aircraft in the fleet at the TPS showed the students the practical differences in handling between various designs.

In this age of computers and sophisticated simulators, there is not a lot of mystique left in flying, but maybe it's still there in test flying. The outsider rarely gets to appreciate the hard work that must be completed before a test pilot emerges from this and the other military test piloting organisations around the world.

It had been a rare privilege to fly with the USAF Test Pilot School, to experience what it is like to be a student at the Test Pilot School, if only for a day . . .

14

Warbird Restoration

Generations of airmen were trained on the AT-6 advanced trainer during the second world war and in subsequent years. North American built over 15,000 of them under the various designations of the AT-6: SNJ; Harvard; and Texan. Across the United States many of the existing AT-6s and SNJs had been painstakingly restored. I had long wanted to fly one of these classic aircraft. Eventually I had the opportunity of flying with John Collver, corporate pilot and fellow Great Lakes afficionado.

John's SNJ-5 squatted pugnaciously on the ramp at Torrance airport on the occasion of our first flight. It was a large aircraft, stretching forty-two feet from wingtip to wingtip and almost twenty-nine feet from the silver dome of its constant speed propeller to the tip of its tail. This big trainer, powered by a 550 hp Pratt & Whitney R-1340-AN1 radial, was immaculately painted in 1950s vintage Marine markings, as aircraft 90917, tail code WD. This aircraft had belonged to the training squadron VMT-2 based at El Toro, less than fifty miles away down the Californian coast. The chrome-yellow cowling and green identification bands on wing and fuselage made it a distinctive aircraft. Since its restoration it had often been seen at airshows on the California circuit, with John at the controls.

It had a fascinating history. Aircraft 90917 was completed at Dallas, first flying on 16 November 1944. It initially served with HQ Squadron 46 at El Toro, later moving to Fleet Air Wing 14 at MCAS Miramar, San Diego in 1946. After overhaul at the end of 1946, 90917 spent the next eight years with various training squadrons in Florida before being retired to the Navy storage centre at Litchfield Park, Arizona. From there it was shipped to Japan among a number of SNJs supplied to the Japanese Maritime Self-Defense Force under the Mutual Defense Air Program. The aircraft served in Japan from 1957 to the mid-1970s when it was stripped of its useful parts and auctioned off to the Kanai-Shoji Co. for the princely sum of $536.91 for scrap.

But in 1978 aircraft restorer Dennis Buehn from California shipped the remains of 917 back to California, where the aircraft was completely restored by Warbirds West at Compton during 1979. It was a pristine example of the carefully restored warbirds now seen so often in California.

We completed the pre-flight and I climbed aboard. The view from the back seat was minimal, bringing back memories of many hours spent in the rear seat of the DHC-1 Chipmunk. Both were taildraggers, so I knew what to expect when taxying. So I strapped into the roomy cockpit, while John ran through the pre-start checks with me.

Any vintage warbird had a fairly complex procedure to get started. By this time I had prepared myself with a lengthy session with the flight manual and the cockpit was not too unfamiliar. John had just brought the aircraft in from its base at Compton. The engine was still hot and needed no priming.

We went through the checks: 'Parking brake on; mixture rich; prop lever to full decrease and throttle a half inch open; carb heat cold; oil cooler open; fuel on reserve tank; battery on; generator on . . .' The litany continued: 'pump the wobble pump until you get four psi on the fuel pressure gauge.' The stick came fully back for starting. Both ignition switches went on the ON position, then John energised and engaged the starter.

The big radial turned over and the prop juddered round. One cylinder fired, sending a blast of blue smoke down the right hand side of the fuselage. The other cylinders fired in turn. As the engine caught the big prop spun into invisibility and the blare of the engine settled down into a steady rumble. Engine pressures and temperatures were OK and at 1,000 rpm oil pressure was satisfactory, indicating eighty psi. We were ready to move. The tailwheel was steered through the rudder pedals, but remaining locked for take-off and landing. John reminded me that I had to push the stick forward to unlock the tailwheel for taxiing.

I got us moving with a burst of power. Cautiously checking the brakes I turned the SNJ along the taxi-way. Taxying out I swung the nose from side to side to check the way ahead as we threaded our way carefully down a none-too-wide taxi-way between rows of parked aircraft. With 5,000lb of aircraft strapped to me, I could feel the inertia trying to swing the tail into an incipient ground loop even at this low speed, so I prudently kept the speed down. I could feel the tailwheel bouncing over the joints in the concrete during taxying, amplified by my sitting well aft of the c.g. of the aircraft.

At the run-up area for runway 29R we turned into wind and performed the pre-take-off checks. A standard CIGFTPR check sufficed: 'Controls free; instruments OK; gas checked on all tanks, then put back on reserve for takeoff; flaps checked for operation and then selected up; trim tabs set, with elevator trim down on my left side set to eleven o'clock and rudder trim to two o'clock. Prop to high rpm . . .' At 1,600 rpm the propeller pitch was cycled, giving a normal 200 rpm drop.

Then the throttle was advanced and as the engine really thundered away the magnetos were checked at 2,200 rpm. We were allowed a 100 rpm drop for each magneto. Within limits. Carburettor heat similarly checked out OK and I throttled back to 1,000 rpm to check that the vacuum was sufficient to keep our gyro instruments humming away. Hydraulics were on and reading just under 1,000lb/square inch. General practice was for both canopies to be cracked open a few inches in case of an emergency during take-off that would require us to exit speedily.

Checks completed, it was time to go.

We got clearance from the tower, and I turned onto the runway, locking the tailwheel once we were pointing straight down the runway. Releasing the brakes I progressively opened the throttle on the left hand quadrant. Full power brought the manifold pressure up to thirty-six inches. I had been expecting a strong swing as we accelerated, but progressive application of right rudder kept things well under control. With my canopy open, the noise was deafening.

At forty knots it was time to ease the stick forward and the tail came up. At seventy knots we lifted off. A touch on the brakes stopped the wheels rotating. It was a busy time while John pushed the hydraulic power lever and raised the gear. By this time we were climbing well and I throttled back to thirty inches of manifold pressure and 2,000 rpm in deference to the tender ears of the homeowners below our flightpath and the even more tender electronic ears of the noise monitoring stations which surrounded Torrance airport. The power reduction helped to minimise the typical blare from the supersonic prop tips so familiar to generations of airmen trained on the SNJ and AT-6.

We climbed out to the practice area. Swinging my rear canopy closed I shut out some of the noise. I found that the controls were well harmonised and with each succeeding minute realised that this was a delightful aircraft to fly. Once we were out over the Pacific I started with a few medium turns, then progressed into steep turns, being rewarded with a bump as we hit our own wake at the conclusion of the first three hundred and sixty degrees. Beginners luck.

The ailerons were delightfully effective. Manoeuvres in pitch were . . . well . . . different. Gentle wingovers were fun but the heavy aircraft certainly lost height quickly. It was just a matter of becoming accustomed to this. My aerobatics of late had been performed in an aircraft only a fraction of the weight of the SNJ.

'Want to try doing it with smoke?' said John. As a display aircraft, this SNJ had a full smoke system. So the smoke went on and I amused myself trying to draw shapes in the sky off the Palos Verdes peninsula.

I found it really required a precise touch to fly this big trainer accurately. When we had completed our session of wingovers and rolls, it was time to come back into level flight. We cruised down the coast with the radial engine rumbling away but all too soon it was time to wheel back over the Los Angeles Harbour and prepare to return to Torrance.

Back over the Vincent Thomas Bridge we set up on finals for the left runway. John was busy talking me through this first time. Gear down at 110 knots, mixture rich and twenty degrees of flap. Bring the speed back to ninety knots on the approach, checking again that the visual indicators on the wing upper surface confirmed that the gear was down. It was time to bring the flaps fully down, maintaining eighty knots on finals. Remembering to put the prop pitch fully forward and watching that airspeed like a hawk. The SNJ had a violent wing drop at the stall, and generations of SNJ pilots had accurate airspeed control drummed into them. It was a busy time.

The left runway was the shorter of the two and we came in low over the rows of hangars at the end of the field, aiming to hit the first few feet of runway. Visibility from the back was abysmal of course.

We touched in a normal three-point landing, stick fully back, with brisk rudder work keeping us straight. I remembered to get the stick forward to unlock the tailwheel before we exited the runway, and was more confident about taxying back, adapting to the weight of this aircraft, but still wary of the large wingspan with so many expensive aircraft parked close to either side.

Once we were back in our parking place, we let the engine cool down at 1,200 rpm with the prop control pulled back to full decrease to get the oil out of the prop dome. Mixture to lean, throttle open and fuel finally off after the engine coughed into silence.

There was a lot to learn in flying a warbird, much more than I could hope to absorb in such a brief first acquaintance with this powerful trainer. This was not a machine for your average weekend pilot, any more than the bigger Mustangs and Corsairs which were the next step in the hierarchy of warbirds in California.

Despite this, the AT-6s and SNJs which proliferated in the USA had a fervent band of followers, owners who swore by their noisy and expensive machines. They raced them, polished them and attended aviation meets in droves. One Civil Air Patrol squadron at Van Nuys, the Condor Squadron, operated a flock of AT-6s and SNJs in USAF and Luftwaffe markings, staging mock battles at airshows. I later flew with the Skytypers operating out of Long Beach and flying a fleet of smartly painted SNJ-2s with military precision, skywriting in formation over the southern California beaches. A corresponding unit of Skytypers operated on the east coast.

These vintage warbirds were the most popular thing around.

15

Flying Heinemann's Hot Rod

Skyhawk! An evocative name indeed. The A-4 Skyhawk had been the mainstay of Navy, Marine and foreign air force light attack squadrons for more than thirty years. During this time the diminutive attack bomber had been known as 'Scooter', 'Tinker Toy', 'Bantam Bomber' and 'Heinemann's Hot Rod' the latter name in honour of its designer, Douglas Chief Engineer Ed Heinemann.

The Skyhawk history was a classic. In January 1952 Ed Heinemann stated that he could build a lightweight interceptor with a weight of 12,000lb. The same principles could be applied to a light attack bomber. The Navy challenged him on this. At that time the US Navy attack bomber specification called for a speed of 500 knots, a combat radius of 300 nautical miles and a maximum allowable weight of 30,000lb. The challenge that Heinemann faced was to produce a lightweight, high performance attack aircraft. The El Segundo team were convinced that they could exceed the specification by ninety knots with an aircraft of half that weight. Others were sceptical. Even as piston-engined AD Skyraiders continued to roll off the line at Douglas's El Segundo plant adjoining Los Angeles international airport, Heineman's team worked on the design of this revolutionary attack aircraft.

Exceptionally rigorous efforts to reduce weight led to a number of innovations, such as integration of much of the avionics, and design of a special 40lb ejection seat. A take-off weight of 14,600lb was achieved, thus vindicating the team. In June the Navy issued a contract for two prototype aircraft. The price was to be less than $1 million for each aircraft.

The design of the Skyhawk stressed the use of simple standard sheet, strip and extrusions. Forgings were almost eliminated. The wing was a one-piece structure, small enough so that it could fit on standard carrier elevators without requiring the complexity of a wing-fold. The 260-square-foot delta wing formed an integral fuel tank, with top and bottom skins machined from single sheets. Spars and stringers were made continuous from tip to tip. To further simplify the structure, the front spar was machined in a single piece, then bent in a heated die. The gear retracted forward, with the main wheels turning through ninety degrees to lie flat in the forward part of the wing.

Following the trend set in the design of the F-4D Skyray, the stick could be extended to increase mechanical advantage to retain manual control in the event of hydraulic system failure. The rear fuselage and tail unit could be removed completely to change the engine.

Douglas test pilot Bob Rahn first flew the XA4D-1 on 22 June 1954. Buffeting of the rear fuselage led to the adoption of a 'sugar scoop' fairing at the base of the fin to smooth the airflow over the rear fuselage. A simple flight test expedient, this was to be retained on all production Skyhawks.

During the Vietnam conflict Skyhawks flew from south-east Asian airfields and carriers to hit targets in North and South Vietnam. The agile Skyhawk proved well suited to the close air support missions. A 300 US gallon buddy refuelling store was developed by the El Segundo team to permit the A4D to double as a tanker. A fixed flight refuelling probe was fitted on the starboard side of the nose of later production Skyhawks.

Over Vietnam this flight refuelling capability of the A-4 proved itself many times in keeping Skyhawks airborne when the carrier's flight deck was temporarily fouled. On occasion 'wet-winging' was practised, when Skyhawks with battle damage and losing fuel were simply plugged into the tanker and continued refuelling all the way back to the carrier.

Ordnance carriage was originally limited to 3,000lb on the centreline and 1,000lb under the wings. In addition to bombs, the Skyhawks could also carry HVARs, tactical nuclear weapons, Zuni or Mighty Mouse rockets, Sidewinder missiles, or Bullpup air-to-surface weapons. A pair of 20mm cannons with drum feed was mounted in the wing roots.

The Blue Angels Navy Demonstration Team for many years used the A-4F version. The Skyhawk proved a popular aircraft, with exceptional control harmonisation, good thrust/weight and engine acceleration. The Blue Angels flew one of the closest formations, stacking their Skyhawks only a couple of feet apart. Very skilful pilots.

A two-seat version, the TA-4F, was produced with the fuselage extended twenty-eight inches and fuselage fuel reduced. The Marines used this in Vietnam as a FASTFAC Forward Air Control aircraft. The orange and white TA-4J was in use as the USN's advanced trainer.

In service the Skyhawk airframe proved very tough and previous versions were consequently in demand for retrofit. In fact the A-4B was turned into the A-4P and -4Q for the Argentine Air Force. These were used extensively in the Falklands conflict of 1982. Sixteen different models were built and the final (2960th) Skyhawk came off the line in February 1979.

By the mid-eighties, the US Marine Corps at El Toro in southern California was one of three squadrons still operating the OA-4M version in the Forward Air Control role. The OA-4M was painted in low-visibility grey. It carried an improved avionics fit in the humped fairing on the top of the fuselage and was liberally sprinkled with antennae.

I was invited by the USMC to fly a practice FAC mission in a Marine

Skyhawk with Lt Col Ed Schriber, Commanding Officer of H&MS-13. The task of the OA-4M Skyhawk being Forward Air Control in VFR conditions, it was primarily used as a high-speed platform for spotting and marking targets.

We briefed for a mission in which Lt-Colonel Schriber was to demonstrate various Forward Air Control tasks, including simulated attacks, and to give me a chance to sample the handling qualities of the Skyhawk. On FAC missions the Skyhawks normally flew with two tanks on the inboard pylons and two smoke marker rockets on the outboard stations. For our mission we carried a single centreline tank. This would give us a total of 6,400lb of fuel for a take-off weight of 19,500lb. Our mission duration of ninety minutes would get us back in the pattern at El Toro for some practice GCAs with 2,000lb of fuel.

After being fitted out with my flight equipment, we walked out to the Skyhawk, one of the A-4s parked amongst the F/A-18 Hornets, RF-4C Phantoms and KC-130 tankers resident at El Toro. A ladder gave me access to the lofty cockpit of the Skyhawk, while Lieutenant-Colonel Schriber pre-flighted the Skyhawk.

Once strapped into the Douglas Escepac ejector seat in the rear cockpit, I had a chance to view the appointments while an air cart wound up the J-52-P-408. Once the engine was running and the groundcrew had checked the control surface movements were OK, we armed the seats by pushing up on the 'headknocker' lever in the headrest. Aptly named, this gained your attention by giving you a smart rap on the head if you forgot to stow it.

Flight instruments and radio control panels were directly in front of me. The FAC aircraft were outfitted with UHF and FM radios to enable communication with the FAC on the ground, the direct air support centre and the airborne strike force simultaneously. By modern standards, the Skyhawk had a simple instrument fit. Navigation was by fifties vintage TACAN. Fuel and instruments occupied the right hand of the panel. With full dual controls in the rear cockpit, there was not a lot of excess space compared with more modern fighters.

With callsign OUTLAW 01 we taxied down to the end of runway 07, canopy still raised to let in some breeze against the oppressive heat of the 80 degree day. As we turned onto the active runway, the canopy was lowered and was locked. Ed Schriber brought the J-52 up to full power and released the brakes. With 11,200lb of thrust thundering behind me, acceleration was rapid and we hit our target at 105 knots as the yellow 6000ft marker flashed past. At 147 knots a firm rearward stick movement raised the nose. I felt the long-stroke gear extend as we rotated. Then we were airborne.

As the gear retracted we started turning left, heading south-west and out over the Pacific towards San Clemente island where we could practice our

80

FAC work. For our airwork, our Navy Controller, callsign BEAVER, allocated us airspace on the 185 TACAN radial of the San Clemente beacon. Once we were en route and level at 12,000 feet, Lieutenant-Colonel Schriber demonstrated the classical handling of the Skyhawk, starting with a clean stall. As our airspeed dropped through 150 knots, medium buffeting started to shake the airframe. I watched the aerodynamically operated slats on the leading edge of the tiny delta wing creep out. Slats on the Skyhawk improved low-speed handling for carrier work, but during ACM or formation flight they had been known to deploy asymmetrically, with dire results. Schriber drily informed me that when the Blue Angels flew their A-4Fs, they wired their slats permanently closed to prevent any unintentional deployment.

We continued to slow down and in heavy buffeting eventually the nose dropped straight ahead in a classic stall. The addition of power and forward stick got us back into level flight. It felt just like a much smaller aircraft. As we accelerated, looking over my shoulder at the wing I could see the slats inching back in.

When the TACAN showed that we had reached our assigned airspace, I tried a few aileron rolls. Roll rate in the Skyhawk proved impressive, well in excess of 200 degrees/second, even though I was not even using full stick deflection. Roll reversals were spectacularly fast. Rolling to ninety degrees of bank when entering a turn from level flight was abrupt and almost instantaneous, although I found that I could easily overpull into buffet. After a few minutes of manoeuvring I started to appreciate how the agility and small size of the Skyhawk made it particularly suitable for FAC work, especially when combined with the low IR signature of the dry J-52.

I extended my repertoire to include wingovers, effortlessly soaring to 21,000 feet and ninety degrees of bank at the apex of the wingover while turning through 180 degrees of heading. Control harmonisation was just right and the Skyhawk was a delight to fly.

As we headed back towards San Clemente island along our TACAN radial, we were flying above scattered alto-cumulus with the Pacific visible below. Barrel rolls to left and right were exhilarating and I found the Skyhawk a viceless aircraft.

We descended towards the island for our first simulated FAC attack, skirting the cloud and levelling at five hundred feet, turning right, with my g-suit squeezing my lower body as the g-force increased. We paralleled the mountainous spine of San Clemente island which rose to 2,000 feet off our port wing with the peaks vanishing into cloud.

We had briefed for a FAC attack with our Initial Point (IP) at China Point. From the complexity of the briefing it was obvious that FAC work required a lot of practice and co-ordination, with the front-seater flying and firing the smoke markers while the back-seater was responsible for mission planning, communications and cueing the pilot to landmarks while travelling at high speed and low altitude.

Extensive pre-flight planning was the key, said Ed Schriber, just as it was in Vietnam. Navigation was by 1:50,000 maps in the target area. The FAC Skyhawk was the pivotal point of the attack mission, and timing was critical to co-ordinate with the other strike forces.

I remembered Schriber's words as China Point slid past the port wing. We accelerated to 350 knots under the stratus overcast. The clock was running down towards zero. There was not much room in the cluttered cockpit to keep track of my folded map and as the coastline streamed past, one indentation of the coastline looked very much like another.

Our target was the distinctive shape of Pyramid Rock on the southern tip of the island. Our radar altimeter sprang to life as we angled in over the coastline, the needle jiggling down from five hundred feet. Peacetime regulations kept us purposely high, and the speed was similarly kept down for my benefit. Wartime would see the Skyhawk approaching at fifty feet and 500 knots for missile avoidance.

Even so, it all happened very fast. The target appeared momentarily over Ed Schriber's helmet before he snapped us into a 4g climb, rolled inverted and pulled the nose down to the target. Pyramid Rock reappeared inverted in the windscreen, expanding visibly. We rolled out smoothly as the clock hit zero. At this point in wartime the smoke rockets would have been on their way. Jinking violently to the right to confuse any ground gunners, we reversed to the left so violently that my helmet bounced off the canopy. A second later we were out low over the beach with the water streaming past below as we made our escape.

During our flight back to El Toro I took the opportunity to regain my breath.

Back on contact with the Controller at El Toro, Ed Schriber completed the first GCA without fuss. I carried out the second GCA, with a less polished performance. It had been some time since I had flown a radar approach. Following the instructions in my earphones I was talked down and this time overshot from overhead the approach lights. A further GCA culminated in a touch-and-go with a firm carrier-type landing, then as the power was brought up the Skyhawk leaped into the air again. We followed this with a couple of tight visual circuits. During the downwind leg, with the humid atmosphere at low level, the air conditioning vents spewed out jets of mist which added a sense of theatre to the cockpit. Our final landing, on cue, was ninety minutes after take-off, with the anticipated 2,000lb of fuel.

Precision was the essence of FAC work. The mission had been a graphic demonstration of how the FAC Squadrons fitted into the overall scheme of things in supporting Marine air power.

16
Sunset Delight

From more than two miles above the desert resort of Palm Springs, I looked down to see streamers of dust being scraped up from the desert floor by near gale-force winds. Directly below me Mount San Jacinto was clear, but ahead lay a deck of clouds stretching westwards towards the Pacific coast. The cloud blocked the mouth of the San Gorgonio valley, the only VFR low level route back home to Los Angeles. Listening to the radio traffic I could hear that the Cherokees and Cessnas were having a hard time fighting the rain and turbulence down in the valley. Having been down there on previous occasions I could sympathise with them. The edge of the cloud was hovering just above the entrance to the valley and it looked dark and dismal in that misty cavern.

But up here in the sunlight on the airway, the Mooney was humming along effortlessly, the turbocharged Lycoming pulling me along so that the DME was clocking off the miles at three miles for every minute. I was heading into the setting sun on Airway Victor 16. On the shadowed panel the glowing amber numerals of the KNS-80 area navigation equipment confidently monitored the Mooney's progress between the waypoints I had programmed into it. Instead of bucking the turbulence at low altitude, my task of flying the airways was one of comparative comfort. I was thankful for the fact.

It was time to change frequency to Coast Approach, who would be monitoring the last part of my IFR flight. My route lay from Palm Springs to Paradise VOR and thence via the Seal Beach VOR, culminating in an ILS approach at my home base at Torrance. I contacted Coast Approach and at their direction started to step down in altitude, constantly adjusting power and tweaking the cowl flaps to keep the engine temperature within limits. The Mooney was prone to engine damage due to thermal shock. I was careful not to cool the engine too quickly.

I was by no means the only aircraft in the sky. Five miles to my right a constant double stream of heavy jets paralleled my course. They were heading for Los Angeles International airport. In turn the airliners were dipping down into the clouds far ahead on the final approach to the airport. To the north the summit of Mount Baldy poked above the cloud deck. On this spring day the mountain was topped with snow. Further north still a tremendous arch of lenticular clouds hung in the sky. This was the awesome Sierra wave.

I was always impressed by the sight of the wave. It meant that away to the north, sailplane pilots had a few hours to ride the wave to altitude. This weather had been forecast. At my weather briefing earlier that day I had learned that a depression over the Pacific was bringing rain to the west coast. This rain stretched in a wide belt from Seattle down to San Francisco. The edge of this weather was promised to come into our area. It looked as if that forecast was correct.

Coast Approach cleared me down to 6,000 feet as I approached Paradise VOR. The cloud cover rose to meet me and as I levelled at 6,000 feet I found myself surfing just over the top of the cloud. There was a rare impression of speed as the Mooney skated over the apparently solid cloud deck. By now the sun was almost on the horizon in front of me, turning the cloud into a golden carpet being pulled past below at breathtaking speed. A beautiful sight.

But I had work to do. With my approach plates for Torrance already on my lap, I checked that the various radio aids were set to the correct frequencies and were operating correctly. I checked my missed approach procedure. Once I started to descend, things would tend to get busy. The art of instrument flying was to be prepared.

The VOR flipped as I crossed Paradise VOR, unseen below the cloud. I retuned the receiver to the Seal Beach VOR. On a heading of 238 degrees on Victor 8 I headed towards Seal Beach.

The radio was busy, my controller at Coast Approach having to deal with a series of commercial jets coming into Long Beach airport some ten miles or so ahead of me. His task was complicated by traffic descending into Orange County airport which lay off to my left. The controller at Coast Approach finally solved his problem by asking me to orbit for spacing while he cleared an MD-80 airliner of PSA into Long Beach. It was not an unusual request. I had been asked to do a 360 on an ILS approach before now. Acknowledging, I banked gently right, putting the Mooney's right wingtip down into the golden carpet of cloud, now deeply furrowed by purple shadows. As I turned, the sun swung round behind my back. On completing the orbit I levelled the wings, heading into the eye of the sun, which was by now half-hidden between low battlements of mist which were tearing past to either side.

It was a moment of magical splendour.

By this time Coast Approach had moved the MD-80 out of my way and the controller now cleared me to descend over Seal Beach.

'Mooney 231 Bravo Sierra. Leaving six for four thousand.'

I was reluctant to leave the beauty of this sunset, but started down, the clouds closing quickly above me. It was dark in the cloud, although smooth for the moment and all the needles were behaving themselves. The lights cast a cosy glow over the panel and the haloes of the navigation lights rode at each wingtip. On the panel the green light of the transponder flashed intermittently as the probing radar beams from the various ground stations interrogated the receiver.

I kept my scan going. Something was not quite right. There it was again. A glimmer of red light from the voltage overload light. Throttled back, the alternator could not keep pace with the electrical load. Another quirk of this aircraft. The Mooney was fast but, like a thoroughbred horse, needed a watchful eye kept on it. I eased the throttle forward fractionally and the light went out. As we passed over the Seal Beach beacon at 4,000 feet the VOR flag flicked from TO to FROM. Coast Approach started to vector me southwest, out over Los Angeles Harbour, where I would pick up the ILS into Torrance.

Coast Approach cleared me down to 2,000 feet, vectoring me round to 300 degrees. The localiser needle started moving in from the side of the dial and I gently corrected until it centred. The clouds were darker down here and raindrops started sliding back across the windscreen. I switched on the landing light, dropped the gear, then the flaps in anticipation of intercepting the glideslope. Switching momentarily to the ATIS frequency I listened to the latest recorded weather at Torrance. Home base had a visibility of one mile in rain, with a 600 foot cloudbase. Just sufficient for an ILS approach.

A blue light started pulsing on the panel, signifying that the Mooney was crossing the outer marker. Completing my pre-landing checks I switched to tower frequency for my final clearance. As the glideslope needle started sliding down from its perch at the top of the dial, I started to descend. With decreasing altitude the air started to get rougher. This was not unexpected. Experience told me that the bumpiness was due to the wind blowing past the Palos Verdes hill, just south of the airport.

Knowing this fact, however, did not make the task of flying the ILS any easier as the needles insisted on jiggling about in the turbulence. As the altitude decreased and the beam got narrower I had to ride this tightrope with tiny corrections, trying to anticipate the movements of the instruments.

Time for a final check of gear and flaps. I eased the mixture forward and put the prop into fine pitch. At fifteen hundred feet the rain hit in earnest with fire-hose intensity. As the altimeter inexorably dropped towards a thousand feet I started looking for the first glimpses of the lights. Nothing yet. If nothing appeared by 300 feet I would have to overshoot.

At 600 feet through the blurred screen the first faint glowing balls of the strobe lights started arrowing towards the runway. Then the runway lights materialised. I went to full flap, sliding in over the green threshold lights to a world of colour once more. The Mooney floated until the main wheels

85

finally touched. It was still raining hard and I was wary of applying the brakes lest the Mooney started to aquaplane.

I sped past the first two turn-offs before the momentum was dissipated, finally braking gently and letting the Mooney roll right to the end of the runway. As the red lights barred my progress I turned off the runway to follow the twin lines of blue lights back towards the tie-down area.

I switched to ground frequency for taxi clearance. It looked as if I was the last one home at this normally busy airport. All other aircraft were tied down, their glistening shapes silhouetted against the street lighting. With a final interchange with the unseen controller – 'Torrance Ground, 31 Bravo Sierra, Goodnight' – I pulled into my parking slot and shut down.

Rain still beat heavily down on the cabin top and I waited for a few minutes until it slackened. Meanwhile I packed my charts into my briefcase in the darkened cockpit, lit by the alternating green and white flash of the airport beacon slanting down through the side window.

The drumming of the rain on the metal skin of the Mooney lessened. Inside the cabin the only noise was the gyros whining down into silence. I slid quickly out of the cabin, locked the door behind me, chocked the wheels and attached the tie-down ropes before making a dash for the car. The rain was strangely warm by European standards. It was late, and I was tired. But the memory of that sunset would linger.

17

The Training Game

My initial flying training was carried out on the DHC-1 Chipmunk, an experience shared by thousands of other Royal Air Force-trained pilots. I had also flown the Chipmunk's predecessor, the Tiger Moth. I had found the Chipmunk to be a delightful aeroplane. Having a fixed undercarriage, fixed pitch propeller and minimal blind flying aids it was a simple aircraft to operate. The Tiger Moth had been even simpler but demanded different flying techniques because of the high drag biplane configuration and the relatively ineffective ailerons. On both aircraft, take-off and landing was an acquired art. The Tiger Moth had a tailskid and no brakes. Landings on wet grass could be exciting. The Chipmunk was another taildragger and I witnessed one or two tyre-squealing ground loops on the runway during my University Air Squadron days.

By the time I learned to fly in the sixties, all-through jet training was already in full swing in RAF Training Command, using the Jet Provost. But back in the fifties the RAF student flew the Chipmunk before transitioning to the Hunting Percival Provost, powered by a 400hp Leonides piston engine. Now that was really moving up in complexity. But by then of course the RAF student pilot had a respectable number of hours under his belt.

At the same time, training in the USA was proceeding along a different track. The USAF student pilot was thrown in at the deep end, starting his flying on the Beech T-34A Mentor. The Mentor had a retractable gear, constant speed propeller and all of 225hp. To my way of thinking this was a big step, but then I had only seen the Mentor in photographs, barely remembering shots of these silver trainers droning over the American heartland. Of course they had long since been retired, to be replaced by the T-37A jet trainer, just as the RAF had gone to all-through jet training on the Jet Provost.

Shortly after arriving in California I had noticed this immaculate T-34A in USAF colours tied down in the transient parking area at Hawthorne airport. I was curious to see a Mentor in the flesh and took time out to walk around the trainer. I had flown a Beech Bonanza and been impressed by the performance. The Mentor had been derived from the Bonanza. I could see the resemblance. The Mentor looked just as it had in those old photos.

Or did it?

At close range this Mentor was not the standard T-34A that I remembered. It had a three-blade propeller instead of the standard two-blader, and it sported a glossy silver-grey Imron paint scheme, while still carrying those 1950 vintage buzz numbers on its fuselage. Closer inspection revealed the small legend N574 on the rear fuselage. This was in fact a lovingly restored and updated version of the Mentor. My curiosity over this civilian-registered aircraft increased greatly.

I eventually met Bob Schindler, owner of this T-34A, who told me the saga of N574. This particular Mentor 55-274 was manufactured by Beech Aircraft in July 1956 as one of the last production batch of 350 Mentors. The T-34A served with the USAF until its training task was eliminated by the introduction of the T-37 during 1960. At this time the T-34As were declared surplus to requirements and made available to USAF Aero Clubs, the Civil Air Patrol and a few civilian owners. No. 55–274 served with the Civil Air Patrol, was eventually declared surplus to requirements and was bought by Bob. He ferried it back from Garland, Texas to Long Beach and started restoring the aircraft.

Bob's photos of the Mentor taken at that time showed a well-used airframe suffering from neglect, with peeling paint giving the aircraft a final touch of weariness. It was not his aim just to restore this machine. A simple restoration would not be enough. Bob had a dream of the precise machine that he wanted to own at the completion of his work. His goal was not to have just a cross-country machine, but a sprightly aerobatic mount.

As the original IO-470-13a in the Mentor was as weary as the airframe, it was replaced by an IO-520b, with this bigger engine driving a new three-blade propeller. Extensive work on the airframe, paint scheme and both cockpit interiors took countless hours over the years before the aircraft was transformed into its current pristine form. At the time when I saw it, Bob was using it to commute from his home in the desert community of Apple Valley into Hawthorne, the nearest airport to LAX, where he flew DC-10s for Western Airlines.

On a windy November day at Apple Valley, my curiosity about this potent trainer was to be satisfied, as Bob had invited me to fly his aircraft. As I strapped in, carefully tightening the parachute straps, then the lap and shoulder straps of the aerobatic harness, I felt again that military atmosphere. The feeling was reinforced by the grey cockpit interior, the crowded panel flanked by switch-laden consoles to either side of the pilot, the floor-mounted stick and a hefty throttle lever mounted amidst a cluster of prop and mixture levers in a quadrant on the left cockpit wall.

I had a momentary struggle to reach down and release the gust lock from the base of the control column. (I should have known. Designers in those days always had at least one trick up their sleeves to catch the first-time student after he had strapped in. The Chipmunk had a floor-mounted fuel selector hidden at the base of the stick.)

Bob was riding shotgun in the rear cockpit and fired up the engine while I retightened my shoulder harness. I slid the canopy forward, shutting out the gusty wind and the propwash from the idling engine. Then I took stock of the situation. Full instrumentation for the complete training task, including instrument flying, was fitted in a logical manner on the wide instrument panel. The seating position was a lot higher than in the Bonanza. Visibility over the nose was good, and the fighter-type sliding canopy gave superb all-round visibility.

I taxied out, nosewheel steering making the task of manoeuvring on the congested ramp an easy one. The civilian instructors at the contract primary flying schools must have been overjoyed at the arrival of the T-34A. The Mentor had replaced the AT-6. I had flown the Marine SNJ version of the AT-6 and could sympathise with the task of teaching students to taxi that unwieldy taildragging monster with its forward view restricted by the great radial cowling. The days of S-turning along taxi-ways vanished forever with the arrival of the T-34A.

Reaching the run-up area at the mid-point of the single Apple Valley runway, I set the parking brake and went carefully through the pre-take-off checks. Fuel selector on the left tank, then from left to right I checked round the still unfamiliar cockpit. Easing up to 1,800 rpm on the power brought a healthy roar from the engine. I checked the magnetos with the big rotary switch on the left hand panel and then cycled the prop. Once assured that everything in the power department was in order I visually checked that the approach was clear, released the parking brake and rolled gently out onto runway 18.

A thirty knot wind was blowing from the south-west across the desert. As I opened the throttle, in deference to the crosswind I held a touch of aileron into wind as we accelerated to prevent the upwind wing from rising.

Acceleration was impressive and I rotated at seventy knots, stabilised in the climb at 100 knots and pulled the power back from twenty-eight inches of manifold pressure, setting up for the climb at twenty-five inches and 2,500 rpm.

The Mentor climbed smoothly, despite areas of choppy air which made it difficult to stabilise the rate of climb. On our flight out to Apple Valley in the Bonanza that morning, we had been pursued by the advance signs of an approaching Pacific storm. Clouds had been increasing and the wind had been constantly rising throughout the morning. It was forecast to get worse.

At 7,500 feet I set up the Mentor in a cruise at a leisurely 145 knots at 2,400 rpm. The aircraft initially tried to climb until I realised that I was subconsciously using the same visual cues that I normally used on the Bonanza. As I was sitting about two feet higher than my seating position in the Bonanza, the nose was now too high. A quick correction on the big knurled trim wheel down by my left knee rectified the situation and we settled down in the cruise over the dried-up river bed of the Mojave River.

The IO-520 rumbled away ahead of me. Fuel flow was down to 14gph in the cruise, making the Mentor a reasonably economical machine for cross-country flying. The cockpit was roomy, even with a parachute restricting the available space. Visibility was impressive and more than adequate for operation out of a crowded training base or for visual navigation.

'Want to try some aerobatics?' Bob asked. 'Do anything you want to apart from snap rolls.' I needed no second bidding.

I started with a loop. As the nose passed the vertical during the climb I looked upwards, past the windscreen arch and up through the canopy in anticipation of the horizon appearing. There was the jagged skyline of the San Gabriel mountains hanging inverted above me, silhouetted against a sky full of ominous lenticular clouds as the approaching frontal system crept in from the Pacific. Airspeed and g-force increased as we dived easily out of the loop, tracking along one of those endless desert roads to keep straight.

Pulling the nose up through the horizon, I checked that the speed was exactly 130 knots, checked the nose at fifteen degrees above the horizon, then pushed the stick over to the left. The Mentor rolled effortlessly and I snapped the stick back to kill the roll rate as the desert floor came level underneath again.

This was fun.

I twisted round in my seat, checking for other traffic. We were clear, but I suddenly realised that I was looking at the stars and bars on the port wing. A look to the right revealed USAF on the starboard wing. Of course. The military trainer. The handling is very like the old Chipmunk after all. In those far-off days I used railway tracks for orientation when flying above the Isle of Wight. My wings then were adorned with roundels instead of the USAF insignia, but the aircraft handling was very similar. The controls were well-harmonised and all the basic manoeuvres were accomplished with no trim changes or unexpected behaviour. Stalls were docile, with just a murmur of pre-stall buffeting before a straight nose drop. Steep turns were enjoyable, those precise ailerons making it easy to roll into the turns. It was all rather exhilarating.

After our brief aerobatic session we descended on a northerly heading for Apple Valley. An encounter with rough air during the descent reminded me that this was a very stable aircraft as the T-34A maintained its trimmed attitude despite the chop. There was none of the directional tail-wagging which we had encountered earlier that day in the V-tailed Bonanza.

Entering the pattern at Apple Valley I set up for a 4,000 foot downwind leg (one thousand feet pattern altitude above field elevation of 3,000 feet) and let the airspeed bleed off to 100 knots. At mid-field I reached forward and pushed the gear handle down. The three magnetic indicators changed in turn from blank to cross-hatched to signify the gear was locked down.

Now with prop fully forward and partial flaps I came round in a curving descent, letting the speed taper off to eighty knots on finals. The windsock still showed a strong crosswind from the right, but the T-34A came down the centreline as if on rails. Touchdown was gentle and there was no problem controlling the aircraft directionally despite the crosswind. As the Mentor tracked down the centreline I advanced the throttle, retracted the flaps and we climbed away again. As the gear locked up, the lamp in the gear handle winked out and the indicators tumbled back to show blank again. In the strong wind we were already almost at pattern altitude as the upwind end of the runway passed beneath the wings. I banked round on to the downwind leg and pushed the gear handle down as we passed mid-field.

This time only two cross-hatched indicators appeared, suggesting that we had only the nose and right main gears locked down. I looked apprehensively at the panel, like a first-time visitor to Las Vegas willing the last window of the fruit machine to produce a winning selection. The third window remained obstinately blank. I mentioned this to Bob, fearing the worst.

'Tap the indicator,' he chuckled. I tentatively tapped the panel and sure enough the reluctant indicator flipped to cross-hatched. I curved round on to finals, in a steeper turning descent now that I was more familiar with the handling. Touchdown was uneventful and we turned off at mid-field. I taxied back to the terminal building, parked in our slot and shut down. As the engine died I slid the canopy back. The gusting desert wind reminded me to slip the control lock into place before disembarking.

As we dashed for the shelter of the terminal building to escape the wind I turned for a last look. The Mentor still looked a purposeful training machine and I had found it a very sprightly aircraft.

The T-34A did not have a long career in the USAF. It was introduced on course 55-M at Marana, Arizona in May 1954 and was phased out in November 1960. This was not a reflection on the design, it was just that the aircraft was overtaken by events. The Mentor originally superseded the AT-6 because of the need for a more suitable trainer for budding jet pilots. Students aiming for qualification as jet-rated pilots in the fifties flew forty hours in the T-34A, followed by 90 hours in the big radial-engined T-28 before graduating to the T-33 jet trainer.

Beech had developed their two-seat military primary trainer from the civil Bonanza. This was the A45 which flew for the first time on 2 December 1948. The USAF acquired three Model 45s, and designated them YT-34, for evaluation and testing at Randolph Field during 1950. The Mentor was subsequently selected as the primary USAF trainer under the designation of T-34A, with three hundred and fifty eventually being produced for the USAF.

But in the training game, through-jet training was the coming thing. Beech saw the writing on the wall and redesigned the Mentor for jet power, flying its model 73 Jet Mentor prototype on 18 December 1955. However it was Cessna who won the contract for the new jet trainer. It was their T-37 which was to shoulder the burden of primary training in Air Training Command from 1961 until the present day.

Other air forces around the world were to continue to fly T-34As for many years. The USN operated their own T-34Bs, then turned to turbine power with the T-34C, using a derated PT-6. The Navy eventually bought a total of 155 T-34Cs and operates them to this day. Not bad for an airframe which basically is a forty-year-old design.

18

Night Owl

Night had long been a cloak of invisibility for military movements on land, sea or air. Radar had its limitations, especially as the radar transmissions acted as a beacon for any enemy missiles to follow. A partial answer was found in the use of night vision goggles which could amplify available starlight. Goggles in turn had their limits, however. For use in the inky blackness of a moonless night under an overcast, various types of Forward-Looking Infra-Red systems (FLIR) were developed. FLIR was passive and did not radiate signals as did radar.

I had flown a daylight mission to assess a FLIR in the unique and strange-looking ASTTA aircraft, a twin-turboprop transport fitted with a radar and FLIR. The acronym ASTTA stood for the Avionics Systems Test Training Aircraft, modified from a Convair 850 transport. The ASTTA was a one-off research aircraft and was flown from a duplicate cockpit back in the cabin. Fitted with a fly-by-wire flight control system, the transport had been modified to fly like a fighter. The FLIR had proved useful during the flight, but of course I only had to look out of the window to see the target in the eighty-mile visibility of the high desert out at Edwards AFB.

Shortly afterwards came an opportunity to fly a real FLIR mission at night with the US Marine Corps. The Marines at Camp Pendleton in California flew a mix of OV-10As and OV-10Ds for Forward Air Control. I had previously flown a tactical mission with the OV-10A in daylight, so was familiar with this twin-boom turboprop.

The North American Rockwell OV-10A was designed as a counter-insurgency aircraft. Airesearch T-76 turboprops of 715hp each gave good acceleration on take-off. When this was combined with the lift improvement given by the double-slotted flap system, a spectacular take-off roll of under eight hundred feet was possible. Counter-rotating propellers eliminated the normal swing on take-off and reversing propellers gave a remarkably short ground run on landing. A long-stroke trailing-link tricycle landing gear mopped up bumps and permitted the Marines to operate their Broncos from roads and primitive airstrips.

In flight, the bulged canopy gave good visibility. The cockpit was spacious and rugged. Reversals and steep turns during tactical manoeuvring confirmed the OV-10's ability to turn on a sixpence, invaluable in the battlefield environment. Even at low speeds the combination of ailerons and spoilers on the upper surface of the wing gave a good roll rate. The Bronco packed a considerable punch. Fixed armament was a quartet of 7.62mm guns mounted in the sponsons under the cockpit. For the normal Forward Air Control task, Zuni rockets or 2.75 inch rockets could be carried for target-marking. The Marine pilots of VMO-2 swore by their Broncos.

The OV-10D was modified for the night surveillance mission. It was distinguished by infra-red suppressors on the exhausts and larger engines of 1040hp each driving new fibreglass propellers. The extended nose of the OV-10D was fitted with a slewable chin turret which mounted a combined FLIR and laser. This system provided automatic target tracking together with laser target designation and ranging. The laser could be used to direct laser-guided munitions such as the Paveway Laser Guided Bomb and the Hellfire missile.

VMO-2 naturally used the night observation capability of the OV-10D as an extension of its daytime capability. For example, the squadron had monitored aircraft suspected of drug smuggling coming up from Mexico. The pilots had been tight-lipped about this, but said that very little could outrun the turboprop Bronco.

At low level under normal starlight conditions, they had found that the best results came when the pilot used night vision goggles for terrain avoidance and pilot navigation, with the back-seater using the FLIR for target identification.

I was briefed on the aircraft system by Major Russ Looney of VMO-2. Sitting in the rear cockpit of our OV-10D on the ground I found the rear cockpit was naturally similar to that of the OV-10A. There were some additions. The FLIR display was a nine-inch screen up on the left coaming. A smaller repeater unit was provided in the front cockpit for the pilot. The electrical load of the FLIR was such that a third inverter had been added. Until the engines were running, the power to activate the FLIR was provided by a ground power unit, sitting on the ramp beside the Bronco, connected to the fuselage by a thick electrical umbilical.

The FLIR display, together with a radar warning display on the right side of the back-seater's instrument panel, detracted from the forward visibility enjoyed by the OV-10A.

I went carefully through the sequence necessary to activate the FLIR, switching on the unit and then going through the various modes, while the ground power unit howled away, providing the power to run the FLIR. The display gave a black and white infra-red picture, similar to a TV. I practised tracking the other Broncos and helicopters moving about the ramp. While the aircraft appeared as various shades of grey, the hotter engine exhausts showed as white.

The back-seater swivelled the FLIR with a hand controller on the right hand side of the cockpit while the laser tracker also mounted in the turret was activated from a hand controller on the left hand panel. As this would keep the back-seater's hands fully occupied, a floor-mounted intercom button could be operated with the left foot while a radio transmit button was operated by his right foot.

As the sun set, we briefed for the mission.

Our night mission, piloted by Lieutenant-Colonel Don Persky, CO of VMO-2, would take us initially round the populated local area to give me some familiarisation with the system. We would then head east towards the mountainous area around Mount Palomar and Lake Henshaw to practise using the system against various targets. The desert of the Borrego valley would be an ideal place to carry out simulated diving gun attacks before heading back to the coast to look for any maritime targets.

Just after sunset we walked out to our olive-drab aircraft, silhouetted menacingly against a western sky glowing eerily with multi-coloured curves and bands of light, the aftermath of a satellite launch from Vandenberg. We strapped into the ejection seats and carried out our respective pre-start checks. The night air was cooling fast and I lost no time in closing down the large transparencies flanking my seat. The panel sprang to life. Once both engines were running I pushed in the inverter control to power up the system and put the FLIR to standby. This started the sequence to cool down the sensors. In a couple of minutes my FLIR display started to brighten up, so that by the time we were ready to taxi my system was fully operative. Switching the FLIR to the manual tracking mode I practised using the hand controller to slew the turret in elevation and azimuth to track a pair of unsuspecting seagulls flying past in the twilight.

With power levers forward and brakes released, the combined 2,080hp of the T-76s smartly accelerated us to our 110 knots lift-off speed. During a lazy left hand orbit after take-off I practised slewing the seeker with the hand controller, easily picking out roads and houses.

We initially headed east to the mountains. By now it was pitch dark, although a moon was rising in the east. Looking over the side I could just make out the hazy blur of the ground, but no details could be seen. Arriving at Lake Henshaw, I looked with the FLIR to see if any boat traffic was visible. In fact, I could see that all the boats had been beached for the night. The display was amazingly clear, so much so that I was surprised to see even the image of the mountains reflected in the lake.

A flashing strobe light at our ten o'clock provided an opportunity of tracking an air-to-air target. Slewing the turret to our nine o'clock, in a wide-angle scan, I found the white dot of the target at the appropriate bearing, heading on a reciprocal course to us. Switching to a telephoto display gave a magnified view of the target, recognisable as an innocent Cherokee heading for

Oceanside. Any Bronco pilot would become a night-fighter ace with no trouble at all.

Further east over the unlit desert we identified a rectangular pattern of solar collectors on the ground. While I kept the turret slewed to this target using the hand controller, then pressed the trigger to lock it on the target, we initially flew away from the target until it was way behind my right shoulder. We then turned through 180 degrees back towards the target for an attack. Despite this manoeuvring the FLIR stayed locked on the target. Range to the target, displayed on the bottom of the screen, started counting down. When the target was at our twelve o'clock I locked the system to the boresight mode. Lt-Col Persky, using his FLIR repeater display, entered a simulated ten degree dive gun attack.

Weapons attacks at night are never routine. Diving into the inky blackness of the Borrego desert with mountainous terrain around is always going to gain your attention. However, with the target displayed on the screen together with its range, and with radar altitude available, it became a much more civilised affair. On the display the target expanded as we dived until a 4g pullout pushed me down in my seat and got us heading back upstairs.

I reset the FLIR in manual tracking mode, searching for more targets in the desert. Initially my attempts at locking on smaller discrete targets were unsuccessful. The trick here was to fiddle with the controls to fine-tune the size of a small rectangular box on the display which had to overlay the target. Choosing the right size was important in achieving lock. My success rate improved as I reduced the size of the box to just encompass the target. In a few minutes I could even lock onto cars driving down the desert roads.

Cruising at 160 knots and 8,700ft we turned west to return to the coast. Locking the FLIR into the boresight mode I took control of the OV-10D for a few minutes to try a few tracking manoeuvres using only the FLIR for reference. The OV-10 had fairly light control forces and was quite responsive. I used my FLIR display, offset on the left hand side of the cockpit, for reference. Despite this offset it was easy enough to pick a ground target and fly the aircraft until the cursor crosshairs overlaid the target in a simulated gun-aiming situation.

While still some miles inland and scanning seaward with the FLIR again, I could clearly see a power station complex on the coast. Anchored some way offshore was a large supertanker, stern-on. I obtained a good lock on this ship. We flew out over the sea while I practised locking-on in various modes. The target was an attack pilot's dream.

We turned inland again and flew back towards Camp Pendleton. Runways and hangars came up clearly on the display. As we ran in to the overhead I practised locking onto an aircraft on the runway. Even when we circled for landing the system maintained lock on this other aircraft as it took off.

We landed, taxying back while using the FLIR in a surveillance mode, proving that it would be possible to steer around the taxi-ways and between other aircraft to our parking space even if the field were to be blacked out. Our ground crew were clearly visible on the display as they marshalled us into our parking spot.

I was mightily impressed. The FLIR system was similar to that used by the Coast Guard to combat contraband smuggling. It was a powerful tool, could see through darkness, haze, or smoke, and multiplied the capability of the aircraft immensely. The Bronco was a handy aircraft. It was apparent that an experienced crew could use the FLIR and laser systems to good effect to carry out observation and ordnance delivery at night. Technology and team-work combined to give this Night Owl a devastating punch.

19
Riding the Friendly Giant

It was a sparkling winter's day and Goodyear Blimp *Columbia* rode serenely at the mooring mast. Here at the Carson base in southern California I was about to be initiated into the world of lighter-than-air flight. *Columbia* was alone and as a fitful wind changed direction, the airship quietly turned, always pointing into wind, trundling on her single castoring wheel round a circular path on the concrete ramp. Heavy shot bags attached to the blue and white passenger gondola kept her helium-filled bulk in equilibrium, and every few minutes the sporadic hum of an electric fan drifted across the field. This fan was automatically topping up the air pressure in the internal ballonets deep within the airship.

A smart blue and white van drove out to the ship apparently grazing at the mast. An overalled figure emerged and went about his tasks preparing the beast for flight. Both engines were topped up with oil, then the blower rig which maintained the envelope ballonet pressure on the ground was disconnected. Moments later the tiny figure climbed aboard the gondola, dwarfed by the sheer size of the airship. One engine coughed into life and the pusher propeller blurred into a silver disc in the sunlight. Then the second engine sprang into life and the field echoed briefly to the blare of sound as the engines were run up. The sound altered as propeller pitch was checked in both forward and reverse pitch before the throttles were pulled back to let the engines idle quietly. It was almost eleven o'clock, time for the first flight of the day.

Without ceremony, more than a dozen Goodyear crewmen materialised from the Operations Building, walked out across the field and took up their positions around the ship. Three men attended each of the two nose-mounted mooring ropes, while others steadied the gondola. *Columbia* was unhitched from the mast and was walked sedately downwind to give room for take-off.

Together with Tom Matus, *Columbia's* pilot, I walked out to the ship. *Columbia* could carry six passengers and we had a full load this morning. The passengers boarded one by one, with the crew removing shot bags to compensate for the weight of each passenger as they boarded. I was last one in, replacing the crewman who had been running the engines. Tom waved me to take the right hand seat at his side. As I took my seat the door was closed and locked behind me.

The interior of the gondola was a cheery place, with a bench seat for three at the rear of the cabin under a brightly painted ballooning mural. A further pair of seats was situated amidships, with our two seats at the forward end of the cabin. After a lifetime of strapping into various flying machines I was mildly surprised to find that there were no seat belts. Still, I reasoned, Goodyear had carried over a million passengers safely, so maybe I was worrying unnecessarily.

Meanwhile, Tom was carrying on a conversation with his crew chief through the open window as the final adjustments were made to the trim by moving shot bags in and out of the compartments located on each side of the gondola. Satisfied with the trim, Tom nodded and the compartment doors were slammed closed, the warning lights on the panel winking out as the doors locked.

We were not yet floating. I realised that although the ground crew was steadying the gondola, our single wheel was still on the ground. Tom told me that normal procedure was for the airship to start off slightly heavy. As fuel was burned off during the morning the ship would become lighter. The heat of the day would increase the helium temperature and make the ship progressively more buoyant.

There was obviously an art to all this lighter-than-air aviating.

It was time to take off. With a concerted motion the crew bounced *Columbia* on her single wheel. As the ship rebounded gently into the air Tom pushed the throttles forward. In a blare of sound the airship accelerated and Tom wound back on the large elevator control wheel to the right of his seat. The nose rose and with the engines at full power we climbed at an impossibly steep angle by aircraft standards.

Engines snarling, with the propeller noise reverberating back from the taut grey fabric of the airship's belly, we climbed rapidly to *Columbia*'s crusing altitude of a thousand feet. Tom pulled back the twin throttles as the nose of the airship still pointed skywards. I instinctively braced for a stall but of course the airship continued to head upwards, slowly pitching down into level flight.

Tom grinned at my discomfiture: 'It gets all fixed wing pilots like that the first time.' I nodded wisely as my heart rate slowly decreased. By now *Columbia* was heading south at a leisurely forty knots. The view was superb from the panoramic windows of the gondola. To our right lay Torrance and the sweep of the Palos Verdes peninsula. In front of us Long Beach Harbour glinted in the sunlight and away to our left the mountains to the north, rimming the Los Angeles Basin, appeared to float with their bases in the morning mist.

Tom let me fly *Columbia*. Sliding into the pilot's seat I took stock of the instruments. The familiar faces of the flight instruments, engine controls and radios I recognised. Others were labelled DAMPER CONTROL,

HELIUM PRESSURE, HELIUM TEMPERATURE. These gauges were strangers to me.

'Let's head down towards Long Beach for a moment,' said Tom. Using my feet on the rudder pedals I tried to target the nose on the distant silver dome housing the Spruce Goose. It lay on the edge of Los Angeles Harbour. Our twin handling ropes dangling beneath the nose started to edge round the horizon towards the dome as I gingerly pushed on one pedal.

Becoming impatient with the lack of results, I pushed harder. Tom grinned and said, 'You'll find it's not like an airplane,' and I wondered why.

An age passed before eventually *Columbia* decided to swing. The nose accelerated past the dome and way off to the far side. My heart sank. This was ridiculous. It took a couple of oscillations before I got the hand of this delayed response and persuaded the nose back on target. There was a knack to it. More like trying to get a grazing elephant to head in the right direction. Gentle persuasion was the name of the game with this friendly giant.

I noticed that the nose had risen slightly as we droned under a small cloud and ran into an area of rising air. In a powered aircraft we would have felt it as turbulence, in a sailplane it would have been classed as a thermal, but here it was no more than a gentle rocking which would be more appropriate to send a baby to sleep in its crib.

Trying to outguess this behemoth I wound the elevator control wheel forward; too far, in fact, and I managed to get the nose well below the horizon. We were now pointing downhill at an oil refinery below us and I felt as if we were about to carry out a dive-bombing attack on the unsuspecting citizens of Wilmington below us. Apprehensively I looked across at Tom, who was unconcernedly chatting with the passengers and pointing out landmarks. It felt to me as if we were plummeting earthwards until I noticed that the altimeter needle was still floating at the thousand foot mark.

It struck me now what Tom had meant when he said 'it doesn't fly like an airplane'. Of course it didn't. Despite having flying controls it was still a balloon, albeit a balloon one hundred and ninety-two feet long. Irrespective of whether I pointed the nose up or down we would float in equilibrium at this altitude, loafing along with engines throttled well back. To climb or descend the engines would have to be used in conjunction with the elevators to power us up or down from this height. With an airship this size, containing one fifth of a million cubic feet of gas, and with a weight of around six tons, the inertia of the ship was significant. It took a bit of getting used to.

While I flew, Tom gave me some background information on the Goodyear airship operations. Since 1917 Goodyear had built more than 300 lighter-than-air craft, and at this time operated four blimps for publicity and camera ship purposes. The three US-based airships were named after yachts which had won the Americas Cup yacht race: *Enterprise* (which won in 1930);

Columbia (yachts with this name won four times between 1871 and 1958); and *America*, winner of the first race in 1851. The last member of the team, airship *Europa*, was normally based in England for the summer and operated from a winter base near Rome.

During the daytime, the blimps were familiar sights at sporting events, being used as aerial platforms to enhance coverage of many sporting events, from the Rose Bowl to the Daytona 500. Each blimp carried a video crew and was a self-contained TV transmitting station with colour video transmission from the blimp being transmitted by microwave to the dish of a ground station. Night-time use was even more spectacular, with a giant computer-controlled electronic billboard on either side of the blimp blinking out animated public service and advertising messages to the world. For this task a generator slung under the gondola of the blimp provided the electricity to power more than three thousand seven hundred lamps. These formed the messages and patterns which appeared in red, green, blue and yellow on each 105-foot-long sign.

In a slow circle we droned almost to the harbour, then curved over the industrial areas, with freeways looking like spaghetti carelessly thrown across the landscape and railroad marshalling yards patterning the ground below. As we turned northwards our nose pointed towards King Harbour on the coast at Redondo Beach. King Harbour was almost a second home to the ship and *Columbia* only weeks before had been solemnly declared the official bird of Redondo Beach.

The airship spent a good deal of its working life over the South Bay and Redondo Beach in particular, even monitoring the local ten-kilometre runs, although its normal working area could extend between San Diego and San Francisco, depending on the job at hand. In 1984 *Columbia* was so busy during the Olympics that she was joined by sister ship *America* for the duration of the games.

The Goodyear Operations field came into sight. We changed seats and Tom took control of his airship again. The field, nestled between two intersecting freeways, looked much smaller from the air than it did before we took off. From our lofty perch I could see the handling crew gathering at the centre of the field. The launching mast had now been folded down out of harm's way, leaving the field clear for us to land. As we approached the field Tom discussed the wind conditions over the radio with his crew chief on the ground. Down on the field a hand-carried windsock showed that the wind down there was from the east. But the wind at our altitude was different, as became apparent from *Columbia*'s drift over the ground. Tom elected to land from the north-west. We circled over the freeway, the huge shadow of the blimp drifting over the cars scurrying below.

Nose down and engines roaring, *Columbia* started to descend. As the airship lurched in the bumpy air at the lower altitude it was a busy time for Tom, who had to use large deflections of wheel and pedals to keep us heading in the right direction. Despite this, everything appeared to happen in slow motion as we threaded our way between thickets of power lines bordering the field. We were settled on our approach when suddenly *Columbia* started drifting sideways.

The wind at ground level had changed again and the tiny hand-held windsock out on the field showed that a southerly wind had sprung up. This wind blew us off course at the most inopportune moment. The ground crew could not catch us this time round. So Tom went forward on the throttles and back on the wheel. *Columbia* climbed away for another approach. We circled the field and came in again. There were no problems this time. As the wind stayed on our nose during the approach the figures of the groundcrew grew larger in the windscreen. Men grabbed the ropes and ran out to either side to steady the ship. With a soft jolt our wheel touched and we were down.

Already the passengers for the next flight, an Australian film crew, were waiting off to one side. At the crew chief's instructions we disembarked, one at a time, each person being replaced in turn by a boarding passenger. In this way the passenger weight aboard the gondola remained approximately constant and *Columbia* did not get too far out of trim. Goodyear ran a slick operation and it was only moments before the door closed behind the last passenger. In a blare of sound *Columbia* climbed away on another flight, showing the Goodyear flag over the South Bay once more.

20
Wild Weasels

Wild Weasel missions started in Vietnam back in 1965 after US forces started to lose aircraft to Soviet-built SA-2 missiles. Aircraft were urgently needed to locate and destroy the radar defence system controlling the SAMs. In the event, F-100s, F-105s and F-4Cs were modified to hunt out these radars electronically.

The Wild Weasels supported strike missions over North Vietnam, going in ahead of the strikes to clear a safe corridor to the target. By detecting and attacking SAM sites along the route, the Weasels forced the SAM operators to turn off their radars in order to survive. The Weasel motto – 'First In, Last Out' – earned them the approbation of their colleagues, but resulted in high loss rates. Their mounts originally were two-seat versions of existing aircraft. Avionics were rudimentary. However, a big upgrade in Wild Weasel capability came with the F-4G Phantom.

The F-4G resulted from an Advanced Wild Weasel programme in the 1970s. Starting with a basic F-4E, a total of 116 F-4Gs was fitted with smokeless engines and had an APR-38 targeting avionics system incorporated. The chin-mounted Vulcan cannon was replaced by a fibreglass fairing containing the avionics of the APR-38 and a number of associated antennae. A total of fifty-two antennae was dotted all over the aircraft.

The result of these modifications was an ability with the APR-38 effectively to determine the bearing and distance to an emitting target by triangulation. This information was presented to the Electronics Warfare Officer (EWO) in the rear seat of the Weasel, who was incarcerated behind wall-to-wall displays for the APR-38. The EWO could designate any target and unleash an attack using anti-radiation missiles to home in on the radar transmissions, or use conventional unguided weapons.

On a clear November day, I flew with the 37th Tactical Fighter Wing at George AFB, near Victorville in southern California, on a Weasel training mission.

This two-ship mission started from the 562nd Tactical Fighter Training Squadron of the 37th Wing. Our lead ship, callsign FERRET 1, was an F-4G flown by the Commanding Officer of the 562nd, Lt-Colonel A.J. Thrush, with Major Mike Esters driving the APR-38. I was to be in the back seat of FERRET 2, an F-4E flown by Major Jack Byrne. Operating as a Hunter/Killer team the F-4G would use its APR-38 to identify and attack the target and the F-4E would deliver the *coup de grâce* by dropping extra ordnance on the target.

FERRET 1 was loaded for bear. It carried four AGM-88A HARM missiles on its underwing pylons, together with a pair of AIM-7s in the aft missile wells. A 600-gallon tank was mounted on the centreline pylon. FERRET 2 carried only a centreline tank with our four empty wing pylons incorporating chaff/flare dispensers. A veteran of the air war in Vietnam, our Phantom sported a red star signifying a MiG kill, dated 1972, on the left intake splitter plate.

I clambered up the ladder to the rear cockpit of the Phantom. Once strapped in and with the engines started I selected our inertial navigation to ALIGN. While the navigation system was aligning, Jack Byrne proceeded through the complex ritual of checking the flying controls with our crew chief. I could hear the litany of checks in my earphones as I reviewed my briefing notes.

Our target would be a radar site in the middle of Area 4W in Panamint Valley. Just west of Death Valley, Panamint Valley contained this gap filler surveillance radar which monitored military traffic from Edwards AFB, the Naval Weapons Center at China Lake and NAS Lemoore in addition to our F-4s from George AFB.

The game plan was for us to fly north at altitude as a pair, then let down in Panamint Valley while Mike Esters in the F-4G carried out his Electronic Order of Battle (EOB) intelligence gathering using the APR-38. This would give range and azimuth to the threat emitter. Both aircraft would then fly the appropriate profile to hit the target. Said Colonel Thrush during briefing 'We may want radars to look at us, so our buddies can be sneaking up on them at low level and dropping bombs on them.'

A flashing green light on my panel told me that the system had finished aligning. This allowed me to switch to NAV on the IN. Now that the system had pin-pointed the Phantom's position on the face of the earth, we could taxi out. With a burst of power the Phantom rumbled forward.

We lowered our canopies during the taxi out. I was careful to check the alignment of my canopy actuating rods under the left hand cockpit rail. A yellow stripe had to line up on the rods, double-checking that the locks were engaged. Phantoms had been known to lose their canopies if the locks were not closed completely.

We reached the arming pad. Hands up on our helmets, clear of any switches, we waited while the crew armed our chaff/flare dispensers and the centreline tank. FERRET 1 went through a more lengthy procedure as each of the four HARMs and the centreline tank had to be armed. In case of an engine failure on take-off, the stores would be kicked off to lighten the load. We reviewed the bird strike procedure. Visors down. Pull back on the stick and get it away from the ground. This drill was not an academic exercise. The wing had suffered three bird strikes within the previous week.

A quartering gusty wind was blowing from our right as we pulled onto the runway. FERRET 1 went into afterburner with a roar that could be heard in our cockpit, then released his brakes and accelerated away at the head of twin tongues of flame. FERRET 2 followed suit ten seconds later, cleaning up after take-off and turning north over the Mojave Desert. We cut the corner to close up into formation. At 17,000 feet and 480 knots TAS our Weasels flew north, then descended along the eastern slopes of the Sierra Nevada. Now flying line abreast, both Phantoms were streaking below the ridgeline, while the pilots mutually warned each other of rocks coming up ahead.

I kept losing sight of the camouflaged shape of FERRET 1 against the wooded hillsides. As we flew north the ground rose under us. The Sierras were snow-covered on this November day and the mountain lakes were starting to freeze over. At this point we were a few minutes early on our schedule and had to wait while our airspace was vacated. Over the radio I could hear CHEETAH flight still practising ACM somewhere above us.

So we circled the snow-capped peak of Mt Whitney, waiting for CHEETAH flight to finish their fight and clear the area. At 14,494ft the mountain was a spectacular sight with the jagged skyline of the snow-covered Sierras stretching to the horizon.

As CHEETAH finished its last engagement we started letting down into the Owens Valley. I attempted to correlate the ground returns on my raw radar display with the view outside. It was a day of unlimited visibility. But I met with little success. At least the F-4G had a computerised display which made life easier for the back-seater.

As CHEETAH flight cleared the area we skimmed over the last range of hills and dropped down into Panamint Valley. Mike Esters in FERRET 1 started calling out range and bearing to the radar site. Tension was rising. As we let down to 500 feet, the desert was whipping past below as our airspeed crept up to 450 knots. It was hard for me to think that this was flying according to peacetime rules. In a wartime situation the Weasels would be down to 300 feet and accelerating to over 500 knots to minimise exposure to ground fire. We blasted on towards the target. For my benefit we flew overhead the radar site, banking so that I could recognise the cluster of white buildings. Operationally, using stand-off weapons, this would not have been necessary. By now the HARMs of FERRET 1 would have homed in on the radar scanner and demolished the target.

Immediately closing up and pulling round to the left we headed north for a pre-planned bomb attack. During our formation turn I noticed something strange about the two shadows of the aircraft as they danced over the scrub-covered desert. Whereas our shadow was trailing the familiar dark plume of exhaust gases from our J-79s, the shadow of FERRET 1 had no such tail. The smokeless engines in the F-4G had at last cured the chronic smoke trail problem which had dogged the Phantom throughout its service life. Sliding out of the turn, the Phantoms widened out with FERRET 1 to our right.

When Mike Esters had achieved the required azimuth and distance from the target now some miles behind us he called 'KILLER!' The word was still ringing in my ears when the scrub-covered landscape of Panamint Valley tilted crazily and the stick came back into my lap. I was left contemplating a g-meter reading 5g. The reading was confirmed by the iron grip of the g-suit around my lower body. My helmet started to force itself down over my eyes and my oxygen mask was sliding down my nose as I struggled to continue breathing. Out of the corner of my eye I could see the ground flashing past.

The turn continued and the inexorable pressure did not let up as I felt myself sliding further down into the ejection seat. Straining against the load, and twisting round to see our partner Phantom, my discomfiture was further magnified by the perspiration dripping into my eyes as we reversed course hard left with FERRET 1 turning into us. Everything was happening very fast through this 180 degree turn. As we rolled out of the turn FERRET 1 was a mile away to our right, streaking low over the rolling terrain and slightly ahead of us. Jack Byrne pushed the throttles briefly into afterburner to get us back into line abreast. Speed crept up to 500 knots TAS. We were really moving.

As briefed, seven miles out from the target Colonel Thrush rocked his wings. Jack Byrne warned me 'Turning!' and racked the Phantom round to the right through ninety degrees at 5g, crossing behind FERRET 1. Ten seconds later we turned ninety degrees left, now paralleling our leader but trailing him. We snapped wings level to see FERRET 1 starting to pull up for his simulated bomb delivery, four miles from the target.

As FERRET 1 rolled inverted and pulled down to the target, Jack Byrne already had a visual on the target. Banking left to get the target on our nose, he pulled up at 4g into our pop-up manoeuvre. Passing 6,500 feet we rolled inverted and pulled. As our trajectory peaked out at 8,000 feet I looked up through the canopy to see the cluster of buildings which was our target.

The nose dropped through the horizon into a twenty degree dive. Momentarily I floated at zero g, then the horizon spun as we rolled upright in the dive, heading down towards the mountain ridges. At 5,000 feet Jack grunted 'Pickling' at the moment when we would drop our imaginary bombs. Just then FERRET 1 scooted out to our right, on the deck. Another 4g pull-out above the radar site squashed me down into my seat, then we were banking hard right, jinking furiously to avoid the anticipated ground fire. FERRET 1 was screaming along ahead of us down a canyon. Our

106

throttles went forward and we regained line abreast formation for our mutual protection during this high speed tactical egress. At this low level it was hot and tiring work.

Exiting the area we climbed to a more economical 20,000 feet for the cruise back to George AFB. Major Byrne handed control of the Phantom to me and I spent an interesting few minutes getting used to the inertia of this heavy fighter and the unfamiliar response of the J-79s.

I was only just getting the hang of it when it was time to hand the Phantom back to its rightful owner. We started letting down for an ILS to George AFB in close formation. Wheels and flaps down, with leading edge slats extended, the Phantoms came down the glideslope like ungainly storks. We carried out a low overshoot as briefed and broke on to the downwind leg, curving round for individual landings in the fierce crosswind, with our drag 'chutes blossoming behind the Phantoms.

There was no doubt in my mind that Wild Weaseling was a challenging way of life.

21
Improving on Perfection

In many fields, excellence is represented by a single name which needs no further explanation. In music it is a Stradivarius, in automobiles it is a Rolls-Royce. In aerobatics it is the Pitts Special.

I had first flown the Pitts Special when taking an advanced aerobatic course just after I arrived in southern California. It was hard work but it was fun. At the end of the course I was left with a lasting impression of the exhilarating performance of this diminutive biplane. The controls were light and the roll rate was phenomenal, equalling that of many high performance military jets. It excelled in inverted flight. I was captivated.

Since then I had flown aerobatics intermittently in a variety of military and civil aircraft and found nothing to approach the handling of the Pitts S-2A.

I had flown a number of S-2As and had fun in all of them. However, the S-2A did have one shortcoming. With two on board the 200hp S-2A would inexorably lose altitude during a training sequence. After a few minutes of aerobatics it was standard practice to break off and climb back to altitude. An inconvenience at best for my type of flying, but a distinct handicap in serious competition.

So the Pitts Aircraft Company of Afton, Wyoming, shoe-horned the 260hp Avco Lycoming AEIO-540-D4A5 six-cylinder engine into the Pitts airframe to give improved vertical performance. The resulting two-seater S-2B had the capability to complete an unlimited aerobatic sequence two-up without losing altitude. The single seater S-2T with the same engine would outfly just about anything.

But was the S-2B much different to fly than the S-2A? I had the opportunity to fly Bill Hare's Pitts S-2B N88EW from Hawthorne Airport in southern California.

During the walk-round Bill pointed out the differences from the S-2A. The engine of course was much bigger and heavier. Consequently the wings and main landing gear had been moved forward five inches to compensate for the c.g. shift. The wings remained the same two-spar spruce construction, top wing of NACA 6400 section and lower wing of 00 series. The wings were of symmetrical section to make inverted flight easier.

I marvelled at the attention to detail. One example could be seen on the inboard side of the airfoil-section strut linking the upper and lower ailerons.

A wire was doped along the length of the inboard side of the strut. Bill explained: 'The older S-2A had round-section struts. This new airfoil-section strut on the S-2B reduces drag, but sideslip causes the strut to produce lift and could cause it to vibrate. The wire effectively spoils the lift and prevents any vibration.'

Bill's S-2B stood noticeably higher off the ground than the regular S-2A, with the pointed spinner almost at eye level. The propeller was an eighty-inch constant speed Hartzell two-blade metal prop. Tightly re-cowled, the engine compartment was all new. The characteristic cheek air outlets at the back of the engine bay were deleted and there was now a controllable cowl-flap in the bottom of the engine compartment for cooling.

Naturally enough, a full inverted fuel and oil system was standard. Minor changes to the centre fuselage included provision for a smoke system tank. The fuselage framework was constructed of welded 4130 steel tube with wooden stringers, together with aluminium top decking and side panels. The fuselage sides were now metal-covered, extending back to the rear cockpit and replacing the fabric and stringer cockpit walls of the earlier models.

On the S-2B the two-seat bubble canopy introduced on later S-2As was now standard. The four ailerons were of symmetrical section with aero-dynamic 'spades' on the lower pair.

Digressing for a moment, I'll explain. As if the roll rate was not fast enough on the regular Pitts to make your eyes water, aerobatic aces had started fitting spades to further increase the roll rate. The spades were basically rectangu-lar metal plates cantilevered forward from the bottom of the lower ailerons. Their function was to provide a degree of aerodynamic balance. As the aile-rons were deflected up, the spades were forced down into the airstream and this in turn helped push the aileron further up. In effect this felt rather like power steering on a car, as the aileron forces in flight were reduced dramat-ically.

N88EW still had that new plane smell, having only fifty hours on the Hobbs meter at the time of our flight. Resplendent in an eye-catching red, white and blue sunburst paint scheme on the upper surfaces, with the under-sides a red and white checkerboard, it squatted on the ramp. Every line was purposeful. This was meant for *fun*.

Strapping into the rear cockpit I found that even with a back-type para-chute I was not unduly constricted. This Pitts was flown solo from the rear cockpit and the front office was less comprehensively equipped, although full dual controls were fitted. Squeezing my six feet plus into small aircraft is sometimes accomplished not without effort, but the Pitts rear cockpit was entirely adequate.

The cockpit layout was familiar, being mainly as I remembered from the S-2A. A hefty throttle lever was mounted on the left hand wall. Mixture and prop plungers protruded from the left side of the panel. The panel had normal VFR instruments, with room for the obligatory Aresti sequence card on the rear panel. One prominent addition was the cowl flap control plunger down on the left hand side of the bucket seat. My rudder and brake pedals were now enclosed in fibreglass tunnels, a precaution to stop them from becoming entangled with the loose strap ends from the front seat. A clear plexiglass floor in the cockpit was there to help with orientation over the ground markers during competition.

Before Bill climbed into the front seat we carefully checked the operation of the sideways opening canopy. I swung it shut and slid it forward an inch or two before it locked home. Bill warned that on the S-2B the canopy had to be positively locked before engine start. An unlocked canopy could be lifted open by the slipstream and slammed into the top wing. At $1,500 for a new canopy, it seemed prudent to follow Bill's bidding.

The engine started easily on the first turn of the key. With the oil pressure in the green I pre-selected ATIS (Automatic Terminal Information Service, standard use in the congested California airspace) and the ground frequencies on the radio, obtained taxi clearance and taxied out.

Information 'Romeo' on ATIS was giving a five knot wind from the west. As we taxied down to runway 25, I learned that the forward view was of course minimal. I had to weave to clear the blind spot ahead where that oversized engine blanked out most of the forward view. Another problem turned out to be trying to keep the speed down without riding the brakes. Even with the throttle fully back the S-2B kept accelerating. I kept the cowl flap closed during taxying to raise engine temperature as quickly as possible.

Under the bubble canopy the temperature was rising rapidly as the sun blazed down on us. I wasted no time in finishing the pre-take-off control checks, then the normal magneto and propeller checks. Checks complete, I punched the radio selector to give the pre-selected tower frequency. There was no other traffic as I requested take-off clearance from Hawthorne's 5,000-foot runway.

Hawthorne is a historic field. The Northrop Flying Wings and F-89s originally flew from here; that was before civilisation encroached on the field. The area around the field was now totally built-up, causing Northrop to switch their flight test activities some ninety miles away to Palmdale. These days Hawthorne is normally restricted to general aviation aircraft with the occasional visiting Warbird or executive jet to enliven proceedings.

The tower cleared me for take-off and I swung out onto the runway, with a last visual check that there was no traffic on finals. I appreciated the bubble canopy here. Rolling forward a couple of feet to straighten the tailwheel, I checked that the brakes were off and smoothly advanced the throttle.

The S-2B leaped forward. My headset cut down the racket of the six-cylinder engine to a throaty growl, but the acceleration was awesome. I needed right rudder to keep straight and barely had time to raise the tail before the Pitts flew itself off the runway.

When we had briefed for the flight, Bill had told me to climb at 100 mph. I pulled the stick back, only to find that the airspeed kept increasing. Finally we stabilised at 100 mph, but in a very steep nose-high attitude. In the absence of other cues the transparent floor panel already proved useful in maintaining reference with the centreline of the runway as it receded rapidly below. Abeam the tower we were already at 900 feet and by the end of the runway we were passing 1,500 feet.

Bill had said that this rocket-like climb gave one unusual advantage operationally. With the Los Angeles TCA extending to the boundary of Hawthorne airport on its northern side, all other aircraft leaving Hawthorne to the north had to circle as they climbed to 2,500 feet overhead the field, before entering the VFR corridor which traversed the TCA. The S-2B could reach this point in a straight climb from take-off.

Levelling from this initial climb at 2,500 feet in less than a minute from brake release, I started breathing again and banked south towards the local aerobatic area over the Pacific, south of the Palos Verdes peninsula. Setting up for cruise with cowl flap one-third open and prop pulled back to 2,400 rpm gave us a comfortable 140 mph with the mixture leaned to give a fuel flow of fifteen gallons per hour. Manifold pressure was back to twenty inches. I gently weaved every few seconds to clear the blind spot ahead. An intercom switch on the panel enabled us to talk without the embarrassment of transmitting inadvertently to the world at large. A boon for training.

I gingerly retrimmed with the lever on the left hand cockpit wall, reminding myself that in a Pitts a sensitive hand was required. Even during that steep climb-out I had been aware that I was overcontrolling with the light ailerons. Now I tried a few exploratory control inputs.

It took a few minutes to re-aquaint myself with the lightness of control of the Pitts. Rudder response seemed even more sensitive than I remembered from the S-2A. Inputs of a quarter of an inch banged the nose to either side, while lateral control was such that merely *thinking* of applying aileron gave a thirty degree bank almost instantaneously. With this sort of response, the days of thought control didn't seem far away at all.

Arriving at the aerobatic area, I checked for other traffic before setting up for our aerobatics. Aerobatic practice in California has its own set of problems. Ideally for this sort of assessment we would fly over the desert, using the straight roads as markers. Here over the ocean occasionally the wakes of yachts or boats could be utilised, but today the Pacific was an unrelenting blue beneath us from horizon to horizon.

111

Initially I set up for a loop using the mountains of Catalina Island, some twenty miles offshore, as a reference in lieu of any conventional markers. After making sure that everything was ship-shape on board, I jiggled the prop control forward to 2,600 rpm and pushed the mixture control to RICH. This day I would use 3,500 feet as a reference altitude. With the TCA extending down to 5,000 feet over us at this point, this gave a buffer zone to stay well below this ceiling.

After a last look around to check for stray Cessnas I dived slightly to 160 mph, pulled back to level flight momentarily and eased back on the stick. My initial effort at a loop proved embarrassingly untidy, as the light elevator forces caused me to oscillate above and below the perfect arc. The g-meter jiggled either side of 3g.

Bill chortled. A subsequent loop proved easier, and I even remembered to open out the loop the correct amount at the top as the speed dropped off. This time we bounced in our own propwash at the bottom of this loop. As we came back into level flight again, the altimeter read exactly at our reference altitude of 3,500 feet.

I progressed to manoeuvres in the rolling plane. Half-rolls proved as precise as in the S-2A. With these magic ailerons it was easy to flip to inverted flight and just play about until you were tired of seeing the world upside-down. I tried a number of full rolls with various amounts of stick. Full roll rate was a mind-blowing 240 degrees/second and the roll happened so quickly that little co-ordination could be achieved. I slowed things down by trying a conventional slow roll, giving me more time to observe what was going on. I found that the controls were well harmonised, with little adverse yaw from the ailerons.

The Pitts flew perfectly, any bobbles in our flight path being due entirely to my rusty techniques. The spades on the ailerons certainly made a difference. Roll rate was even higher than the S-2A and rolling was no effort at all compared to the Great Lakes biplane which I had previously been flying.

Inverted flight proved to be simple and comfortable, with the five-point aerobatic harness and back-up lap-belt giving confidence-inspiring support to my lower body. It made a change to fly prolonged inverted manoeuvres without the necessity of having the straps so tight that the circulation to my legs was cut off altogether.

Upright once more, I progressed to Cuban eights. I initiated the manoeuvre from 170 mph, pulling round the loop and over the top, waiting until we were inverted in a forty-five degree dive before rolling upright. No problems here and I repeated the manoeuvre to complete the Cuban Eight. I tried it again, perfecting my timing on the roll-out to equalise the inverted and upright segments of the dive.

It all felt very natural and for variety I tried a couple of reverse Cuban eights, pulling up to forty-five degrees before rolling inverted and pulling through.

'Look at your altitude,' said Bill. Sure enough, at the end of this sequence, our altitude was still basically 3,500 feet and at fifty-five per cent power the AEIO-540 was not even breathing hard.

This was all rather fun. I spent a few minutes trying to perfect my stall turns, managing to do a reasonably tidy manoeuvre but finding a consistent vertical line on the exit elusive. However, it eventually came together. Once back in level flight I even remembered how to do the odd inverted turn without disgracing myself. The Pitts did it all without hesitation.

Bill remarked from the front cockpit that time was getting on and we had better check the fuel remaining. I reluctantly rolled the Pitts upright.

The S-2B is limited to fifteen gallons of fuel with two on board to keep away from the aft c.g. limit. So aerobatic sorties are limited to somewhat less than an hour.

Our manoeuvring had consumed a fair amount of gasoline, so after repeating a few manoeuvres it was time to head back to Hawthorne. With the blunt nose pointed north, the whole of the LA Basin was spread out on this clear morning, with Mount Wilson visible through the shimmer of the prop and the whole of the San Gabriel mountain range athwart our path. We coasted inland over the Palos Verdes peninsula, past the white golf balls of the LAX radar on the hill below. Maintaining 3,000 feet we overflew the traffic pattern at Torrance airport, then started downhill towards Hawthorne over the urban sprawl of the South Bay.

I was impressed by this machine. When Curtis Pitts first came out with his diminutive 90hp single-seater in 1944, little could he imagine that forty years down the road his design would still be in production. But the basic Pitts Special had been constantly refined to produce a stable of factory and home-built variants of progressively greater power and performance, culminating in the potent machine I was flying.

First appearing in September 1982, the S-2B took first place in the Advanced Category at the US Nationals held at Sherman, Texas that same year. The pilot was Clint McHenry and the unusual part of the story was that McHenry carried a passenger, having had his first-class medical pulled by the FAA and getting permission from the authorities to compete only on the condition that he flew with a safety pilot. An impressive performance for both plane and pilot.

As the white strip of the Hawthorne runway came into view, I checked ATIS, then hit the switch for tower frequency to obtain clearance to land. Down to 1,200 feet I set up a downwind leg at 100 mph for runway 25, turning tightly round on to finals. When flying a Pitts, final approach is per-formed either in a tight continuous turn or a sideslip in order to keep the runway in view for the longest possible time. We had traffic in front of us, so I set up a straight-in approach, cross-controlling with stick and rudder to give some sideslip. It seemed easier than in the S-2A. With more headroom under the big bubble canopy I could see further along the side of the nose.

As expected, the runway disappeared under the nose as I scooted in over the fence and I killed the sideslip. As the nose swung to point down the runway I eased the stick back to flare. The Pitts adopted a three-point attitude and there was a momentary hesitation. I had not got the stick quite far enough back. We touched prematurely on the main wheels. The wheels skipped an instant before the tailwheel hit the ground and then we were rumbling down the rather rough runway at Hawthorne. Keeping straight required some dexterous footwork. Just the same as the S-2A, and one of the penalties of attaining the superlative aerobatic performance of the Pitts aircraft.

This was a short flight and one in which I did not explore the furthest reaches of the flight envelope of this aircraft. The g-meter after flight gave evidence of only +4.6 and −1.5g, well within the +6 and −3g placarded limits of the Pitts. Flying a Pitts well requires constant practice. A single flight could do no more than scratch the surface. In the hands of an expert a Pitts could dazzle an airshow audience or hold its own with the latest aerobatic competition monoplanes. During the eighties, expatriate Englishman Ian Padden flew his single-seat S-2T at southern California airshows, and torque rolls, tailslides and multiple snaps were all in a day's work for Ian. Whether single- or two-seaters, the Pitts Special was still a name to be reckoned with. The S-2A had been fun. The S-2B was improving on perfection.

22

Grounded

The trouble started one morning while I was shaving. Suddenly I was aware that I could not hear my watch ticking. The watch sat in its normal position on the tiled surface adjacent to the washbasin. I lifted the watch up, shook it and checked that it was running. Sure enough the second hand was still marching round the dial. But I could not hear it. Puzzled, I held the watch to my left ear. Yes, the watch was ticking, albeit faintly. Still framed in shaving cream, the face in the mirror looked back at me with a puzzled expression.

Had I gone deaf?

Yes. Overnight I had apparently gone deaf in my left ear. Worried now, I held the watch up by my right ear. Again, as I moved the watch closer I could hear a faint ticking. It was slightly louder than the other ear, but nothing like the normal ticking.

Then I remembered. A week or so previously I had been suffering from a cold. This temporary deafness was probably no more than the lingering effects of the cold. Thus rationalised, the problem seemed of little concern. I finished my shave and went downstairs to breakfast.

Later that week I was flying again. I had no problems with my ears during climbs or descents. However, when the deafness showed no signs of clearing up, I began to get concerned and went to see an ear specialist.

After a battery of hearing tests, the results came back. The specialist informed me that I was suffering from progressive otosclerosis in both ears. Basically the problem was calcification of the chain of tiny bones in the middle ear. Instead of vibrating as normal to transmit sound, the bones were slowly but surely fusing together. The process was irreversible, and eventually I would go completely deaf.

For a time the situation was manageable while I was flying. I simply turned up the volume of the radio and could hear the controllers perfectly well. However, on the ground the situation in day-to-day living was increasingly frustrating as my hearing deteriorated. I could not hear telephone messages, conversation became increasingly difficult and my wife and family suffered as my deafness got worse.

In front of me loomed the frightening prospect of complete deafness. I was still flying, but it was rapidly becoming apparent that I would soon be requiring the volume on the radio turned up to its maximum. I was increasingly worried that despite having the radio turned up to full volume, I would miss a vital message from Air Traffic Control, so presenting a risk to others as well as myself. Whichever way I argued to myself, my assessment was that the risk was getting too high. There was no way out.

I reluctantly quit flying.

Others must have gone down this path before me, but it did not make life any easier. In all other respects I was still fit to fly. In my work I was still surrounded by aircraft. Every day I was still working with engineers and pilots. But the uncertainties kept multiplying. Could I ever get back to flying? Even on the ground my future was uncertain. How long would I still be able to continue in my line of work, where teamwork was everything?

There were ways to compensate. I could still write. I experimented with painting. My family were supportive, and we did many things as a family which were still valuable, but there still seemed no way of properly compensating for the loss of an important part of my life.

Then came a ray of hope. A relative of a colleague of mine had suffered from a similar loss of hearing. She had been treated at the House Ear Institute in Los Angeles and treatment had resulted in a dramatic improvement in her hearing.

I arranged to travel to downtown Los Angeles and visited the Institute where I had still more hearing tests. At the Institute my consultant, Dr James Sheehy, said that there was a good chance that the condition could be rectified. The otosclerosis could be treated by removing the offending stapes bones in each ear and replacing them with metal prostheses. This stapedectomy operation had been pioneered by the House Institute and there was a high probability of success. There was a cautionary note, he added: some people were prone to balance problems after the operation.

This latter part was not good news. Balance problems would be the death knell for flying for me.

Still, this was the only long-term solution that presented itself. So I agreed to the proposed treatment. Dr Sheehy explained that the technique was still fairly recent. He would perform two separate operations, one on each ear. There would be a wait of a year before the second operation just to make sure that the first operation was a success.

An appointment for my operation was arranged. My wife drove me to the hospital for Dr Sheehy to operate on my left ear. I am not at ease in hospitals. To compound my discomfort this operation was to be carried out under local anaesthetic. It was all rather unnerving as I was conscious throughout and aware of the surgeon's progress during this delicate operation. My overwhelming worry, as I lay on the operating table, was the need not to sneeze at an inappropriate time during the delicate microsurgery.

The House Institute was host to a constant stream of doctors from all over

116

the world, intent on observing how this new procedure was carried out. So the progress of the operation was monitored by TV cameras for the benefit of this captive audience. Dr Sheehy was terribly cheerful throughout and kept up a running commentary for the benefit of the observers.

All apparently went well and I was kept in the hospital overnight as standard procedure. It was usual, said Dr Sheehy, for one's balance to be a little adrift for a while after the operation. Sure enough, I had to move a bit carefully for a few days. Sudden movements caused strange effects to my inner ear. But as soon as the post-operative swelling had gone down and the dressings were removed, with elation I noticed an improvement in my hearing.

Coming back from deafness was like coming back from a dark tunnel into the light. I could hear 'phones ringing, birds singing and could carry on a normal conversation once more.

It was like being reborn.

As time went on, my hearing improved further in my left ear. It appeared as if things were going OK so far and I waited impatiently for the year to be up so that I could have the fading hearing in my right ear rectified.

The second operation was a mirror image of the first. Again after a few days there was a perceptible improvement in the hearing of my right ear. About a month after the operation I was checked out by Dr Sheehy and his staff and given a clean bill of health. My hearing was back to normal.

By this time I was driving around California again, had started running again to keep in shape, and had encountered no problems. Life on the ground was fine again.

But for me there was one big hurdle to cross. Could I still fly?

My first flight was as a passenger in a twin-engined turboprop. There were no problems, and my balance seemed OK during gentle manoeuvring.

Progress seemed good, but there was no way on earth to duplicate the complex effects on my inner ear that aerobatics would impose, short of actually flying. So I had to bite the bullet and try flying the Great Lakes biplane, with another pilot in the second seat to take over just in case things should go drastically wrong.

It was a beautiful California day when at five thousand feet over the Pacific Ocean, with the wind battering around the open cockpit, I banked the big biplane in a series of clearing turns. Emotionally, I was not at all sure if I wanted to find out the answer to my problem. If my balance was affected, I would have to ground myself permanently. I turned again, ostensibly checking for other aerial traffic but in fact trying to postpone the fateful moment. Everything was very clear as I circled. The sun reflected from the struts, sparkled from the windshield and the shadows swung across the instrument panel as the biplane droned through the California sky.

Eventually I could not think of a reason to prolong the turn further and I took a deep breath, rolled into a bank, let the nose drop into a dive, and started into a loop, the first manoeuvre in my sequence of aerobatics.

Thirty minutes later we landed after thoroughly wringing out the Great Lakes and my vestibular system in a series of aerobatics which included loops rolls, stall turns and spins. As the propeller jerked to a halt I had a grin from ear to ear which needed no explanation. I was back in business.

Later that week I flew again, solo this time, and got back into aerobatic practice after a few flights. Life was good. I was back to normal and flying was even sweeter after this enforced period on the ground.

23

The Time Machine

One of the delights of visiting Edwards Air Force Base was the opportunity to fly in a variety of unusual aircraft. One of these was the Avionics System Test Training Aircraft (ASTTA) operated by a specialised flight test support company, Arvin Calspan of Buffalo, New York. Basically the ASTTA was an in-flight simulator. Starting life as a piston-engined Convair airliner this beast now had turboprop engines, extra side force controller fins part-way out along the wings and a prominent proboscis containing a radar.

However the most radical modifications to the aircraft were only to be found on climbing aboard. In addition to the regular cockpit up front, the ASTTA was equipped with an extra cockpit inside the cabin. Here the students from the Test Pilot School could familiarise themselves with the new systems such as infra-red targetting devices and various types of radar.

There was more. Back in the blacked-out cabin the student also had a sidestick controller, similar to that in the F-16. Using his controls, coupled to a sophisticated fly-by-wire flight control system, he could fly the big machine on instruments as he would a normal fighter.

For my flight Calspan pilot John Ball, up front in the regular cockpit, took off in the normal way and set us up for cruise before engaging the fly-by-wire system and turning control of the machine over to the student in the back. Thereafter he acted as safety pilot, and monitored the panel of lights signifying the operation of the flight control system. Ball could override the system if things started getting out of hand.

We flew on a brilliant autumn day, operating against a T-38 which was scheduled to carry out a series of head-on passes against us so that the students in the cabin could in turn practise acquiring targets on the radar and IR scopes in the cabin. From the cockpit I could hear the reports of target range and distance coming from the cabin. As the range closed a dot ahead would grow rapidly into the T-38 which would whistle past, then turn to set up for another run.

With the air-to-air sequence completed, we flew over to one of the ground ranges in the desert to assess the problems of acquiring ground targets using the IR and radar systems. It was absorbing work, and the safety pilot and the relatively low cruising speed of 180 knots gave more time to appreciate what was happening throughout each run, and was also safer than if the students had been trying to fly an F-16 at 400 knots while assessing the system. By the end of the flight I was thoroughly convinced that this was a cost-effective way of training pilots in systems assessment.

Systems testing was only a part of the syllabus at the Test Pilot School. The classic test pilot role of stick and rudder work to assess aircraft handling was a different matter.

Training test pilots in the assessment of aircraft handling qualities is a difficult task. Student test pilots can be exposed to a variety of aircraft, but this only provides experience on aircraft which have already been through a flight test development programme and had most of the bugs ironed out. The problems can be covered in the classroom, but teaching the pilot to recognise the same problem in flight, and then to deal with it in the appropriate manner, is not easy. If the aircraft turns out to be unstable, it could be downright dangerous.

Ground-based simulators can go part of the way to assess the behaviour of an aircraft prior to flight, but the subtleties of the flight environment make it desirable to use an in-flight simulator to achieve a realistic cockpit environment.

In order to provide a safe demonstration of the various aspects of aircraft handling qualities in flight, Calspan had modified a Learjet 24 with a Variable Stability System. This Learjet was operated under contract to the USAF Test Pilot School at Edwards AFB and also flew for the Navy Test Pilot School at Patuxent River, Maryland.

Calspan and the Air Force invited me to fly the Learjet at Edwards AFB. During the forty-six-week course at the Test Pilot School the student test pilots and flight test engineers flew three flights on the Learjet. The first flight demonstrated the various stability and control parameters associated with longitudinal stability. On the second flight lateral-directional handling was covered. The third was a review flight where the student was exposed to an unknown configuration and could assess and identify the problem.

This workload, in addition to other Calspan flight commitments, kept the Calspan pilots busy, with the three pilots rotating between the Learjet, ASTTA and a variable stability NT-33A. As a result they spent a lot of time on the road, completing a two-week stint at each location before moving to their next assignment. It took some time before our schedules could mesh. I read up avidly on the aircraft.

This Learjet 24 was converted into a variable stability aircraft by the Calspan Flight Research Department under joint funding from the USAF and Navy Test Pilot Schools.

The evaluation pilot's station at the right hand seat was fitted with a fly-by-wire flight control system which coupled on-board computers to electro-hydraulic servo-actuators on the control surfaces. Meanwhile the left-seat safety pilot's control system remained directly connected to the aircraft control surfaces and reflected the commanded surface movements during simulation.

The system could be manually disengaged by either pilot at any time, when the aircraft reverted to the basic Learjet handling for operation by the safety pilot. A safety-trip system was incorporated so that whenever pre-set limits were exceeded, the simulation system would trip out, with the aircraft reverting to the control of the safety pilot.

So here we had the ability to simulate hundreds of different aircraft, with their handling quirks, together with the ability to fly any future aircraft a designer could dream up. And do it in safety. In all there were 128 pre-programmed configurations readily accessed in-flight together with another 128 configurations that could be punched in during flight.

This Learjet had an awesome capability.

I briefed for the flight at the Test Pilot School at Edwards Air Force Base. Calspan pilot Jim Baker was a former Navy test pilot whose qualifications included having a medical degree which led to him spending four years at the Institute of Aviation Medicine at Farnborough. But flying proved more fun than doctoring, so here he was, flying the Learjet and the other Calspan research aircraft.

We briefed for a demonstration flight, due to be airborne at 1430 hours. This would be Baker's third flight that day, the TPS having started their flights in the early morning to ensure the calmest air for test work.

During our pre-flight walk around the sleek red and white jet, Baker pointed out the two extra angle-of-attack sensors on the nose which characterised N101VS from the standard Lear 24. These sensors, together with a sideslip vane under the nose of the aircraft, fed the computers for the Variable Stability System (VSS) whose electronics filled the rear part of the cabin. Baker would be in the left hand seat and I would occupy the right hand seat as the evaluation pilot.

Once we were installed, with the cabin door left open for the moment to keep some air circulating in the ninety degree afternoon, Baker pointed out the cockpit differences from a standard Lear. The VSS was controlled by two panels, one being a gain-change panel and keyboard located on a console between the pilots' seats, the other being on the left hand cockpit side wall. The main instrument panel contained meters displaying pitch, roll and yaw angles. Red sectors on the meters showed the limits at which the system would trip. If things got out of hand, either pilot could disconnect the system independently. The trip warnings and VSS reset buttons were in front of Jim Baker. My panel was that of a standard Learjet with the addition of a meter showing stick-force per g.

While Baker retained the yoke which operated the standard Lear cable-operated flight control system, I had a fighter-type stick operated by the VSS which was connected solely by electronics to the control surfaces.

The cabin door was slammed closed and we were ready to go. Once both engines were running, Jim Baker checked the VSS and the fly-by-wire (FBW) system to ensure that control could be maintained from the right seat in case of safety pilot incapacitation. As always, the greatest danger was from bird strike, the Lear being limited to 306 knots below 14,000 feet through wind-screen bird strike considerations. In the event of a bird strike putting Baker out of action I could re-engage the system simply by hitting the FBW switch and the three FEEL, PRESS and ENGAGE buttons on the instrument panel to regain control.

Having checked that the VSS was serviceable, Baker engaged nosewheel steering and got us moving. The nose dipped as he checked the brakes. With callsign COBRA 37 we were cleared to Runway 22. We taxied down the Edwards ramp past the T-38s, A-7s and F-4s of the TPS and past the B-1s and their chase F-111s. Once lined up on Runway 22, Baker increased power, carried out a power check at eighty per cent and released the brakes. Acceleration was rapid and we rotated at 125 knots. Once established in the climb, Baker pulled the power back to ninety-five per cent and engaged the VSS.

We climbed out over Lake Isabella, got clearance to enter the military airspace known as Eddie 2, north-west of Edwards over the Sierra Nevada, and set up in the cruise at 240 knots and 16,000 feet.

As we whistled on over the rugged mountains, I played the role of a student test pilot. Jim Baker started our demonstration of longitudinal handling with the aircraft set up with positive static stability, as in the standard Learjet.

Initially we looked at the long-period oscillation or phugoid. This standard flight test manoeuvre was entered by pulling the nose up to twenty degrees then releasing the stick, at the same time punching the stopwatch on the panel. The aircraft arced up into the sky, trading speed for height. As the Lear's nose came down to the horizon, speed had dropped to 190 knots. Then the nose continued to drop and we headed for the mountains. We kept our hands on our knees.

After a few seconds the positive stability of the Learjet caused the aircraft to self-recover from the dive and the manoeuvre bottomed out at 280 knots and 14,800 feet. As we passed through 16,000 feet having completed one full cycle, seventy seconds had elapsed. The subsequent oscillations diminished in amplitude and the Learjet gradually regained level flight as the motion damped out. A graphic example of textbook behaviour.

The short period mode was next to be assessed. This is of vital importance in the design of any aircraft. Jim Baker had briefed that we would start by carrying out a frequency sweep in pitch, initially moving the stick fore and aft slowly and gradually increasing frequency. At the resonant frequency the aircraft would exhibit the maximum response. A sharp fore-and-aft input on the control stick at that frequency would excite the Short Period Oscillation. Sure enough, when the stick was pulsed, the aircraft nose oscillated up and down twice, then the motion rapidly damped out, confirming the positive damping of the basic Learjet.

To see how this affected the piloting task during a representative attack manoeuvre, we would attempt to acquire and track a ground target. With a grin Baker said, 'Here we use Calspan's five-cent bombsight.' He was referring to a tape cross on the windshield in front of the right hand seat. Picking a spot on the mountains below, Baker banked the Learjet past the vertical, pulling back on the yoke to roll into a typical ground attack manoeuvre, demonstrating the technique of changing his aim point to various targets during the dive. It was apparent that the basic Learjet's response was sluggish compared with a regular attack aircraft, as he attempted to track four separate targets during the dive.

Back at 16,000 feet in level flight, Jim Baker then reduced the damping ratio. The aircraft started to behave in a squirrely fashion. Pitch disturbances after the fore-and-aft stick input now took five oscillations to damp out. It felt like driving an old car with ineffective shock absorbers. As we headed downhill for the mountains in our attack manoeuvre, it was noticeably harder to track the target, with the nose overshooting each time. During this oscillatory manoeuvre we reached a lower limit of .15g and the VSS system tripped out, illuminating the panel in a blaze of warning lights.

Once back at 16,000 feet and with the VSS once more engaged, Baker then set up zero damping. The aircraft was still stable but with the lack of damping the handling was disastrous. Not only was it virtually impossible to aim the aircraft, but it was all too easy to excite a Pilot Induced Oscillation (PIO); I had a wholesome respect for PIOs, having seen film of an F-4 Phantom come apart during a high speed pass when a PIO developed. But all was not lost. Even though the motion was violent, Baker demonstrated how the aircraft could be recovered from the PIO by catching the oscillation at the top or bottom of the manoeuvre.

Baker now increased the damping ratio. This changed the character of the motion completely, the heavily damped motion giving no overshoots but resulting in a sluggish feel to the aircraft. 'Like trying to carry out ground attacks in a B-52,' one Edwards test pilot, Colonel Bob Behler, said subsequently of this configuration.

Having reached the northern end of our allotted area, we turned just south-west of Owens Lake and set off back over the rugged Sierra Nevada.

The next phase of the assessment was to show the effect of varying the centre of gravity position. This was done electronically by feeding in an angle of attack value from those extra sensors on the nose. With damping restored to the standard Lear value and the c.g. now artificially shifted forward, the normal stick force gradient of 8lb/g had increased to 16lb/g. When the stick was pulsed fore and aft to excite the short period oscillation, the frequency of the motion increased and damping went down, giving five oscillations of the nose before we were back in level flight. This felt pretty weird.

Here we had drastically changed the damping of the motion simply by moving the c.g. forward. Baker stressed that the task of the test pilot was to observe, not to try and analyse the motion which could have a number of parameters varying due to one specific change.

Baker than adjusted the VSS to move the c.g. back to the aft limit. This gave lighter stick forces, although the other flying qualities remained conventional.

When the centre of gravity was moved further aft still, flight characteristics changed markedly. As I pulled the stick back, tracking was still possible but there was no speed stability or speed cues. In this configuration, as I pulled back on the stick the nose just kept pitching up at a constant rate.

With the c.g. further aft still an aft deflection of the stick resulted in the Learjet pitching up to a constant 1.8g. Stick deflection was now giving a pitch acceleration and in this case stick forces had decreased to zero. This felt most uncomfortable . . . like balancing on the head of a pin.

I had heard that a Sopwith Camel was like this. With no stability, it could turn in a flash in combat, but killed many an unwary pilot in doing so. Seventy years on, flying this time machine, I was learning what it must have been like.

Flying cautiously, I determined that it was just possible to fly and manoeuvre the Lear in this condition but it was ever so easy to get it into a PIO. As I deliberately initiated larger inputs to simulate a landing approach, the aircraft started to oscillate in pitch. The motion became divergent. I was too late in clamping the stick and the VSS tripped out as the aircraft went below zero g-force during the oscillation and I floated up against my seatbelt. Luckily Calspan does not carry paying passengers during these flights.

This was a challenge. Licking my lips, when the VSS had been reset I repeated the sequence and this time after I had let the PIO develop I caught it at the top of the oscillation by applying steady back pressure each time the nose started to drop. This was successful in damping the motion and showed the advantage of being able to teach recovery from what would be a dangerous situation if inadvertently encountered in flight.

Flushed with success I repeated the exercise and deliberately initiated a PIO, trying to catch it this time at the bottom of the oscillation. This proved more difficult. As the nose dropped, mountain peaks filled the windscreen and again the system tripped before I could control the motion. I was doubtful that the aircraft could be landed in this configuration.

Baker then returned the system to the basic Lear characteristics to demonstrate the effect of varying the stick force gradient from the 8lb/g of the basic Lear over a range between a bomber-like 25lb/g and a gradient of 2lb/g (almost like the Pitts). Again, tracking was difficult at the heavy end, when during manoeuvres it was necessary to maintain a 50lb force with one hand, and uncomfortably responsive at the light end. It was a strange sensation one moment to be flying a heavy aircraft, then the next to be flying a sensitive aerobatic aircraft.

'Have you ever flown an F-16?' Baker asked. I had to admit I had not. 'This next configuration gives a fixed stick,' he explained, punching in another combination of gains on his panel. 'Early F-16s flew with this system. See how pilot performance is affected. It's very sensitive.'

In this condition my stick was locked and the Lear responded briskly to the lightest pressures on the stick. This was similar to the way the flight control system on the F-16 was set up initially. I had seen film of the prototype getting into a roll-axis PIO during a high-speed taxi run. The pilot had chosen to pull it off the ground to resolve the situation, resulting in an inadvertent first flight of that aircraft. Sure enough, as I cautiously tried tracking manoeuvres on a puffy cumulus cloud, this led to some bobbling in pitch as I got used to this ultra-sensitive system.

Baker added a small degree of motion to the stick. This greatly improved the response and was in fact the solution adopted on later F-16s. He punched in a few more gain changes to further increase the stick deflection. My comment was that it now felt like a sailplane where the resulting control was loose, adequate for thermalling, but not good enough for tracking.

Baker then wound up the friction force electronically. This proved awkward for tracking. Pre-loading the stick back to neutral with a simulated centreing spring to oppose the friction improved matters considerably.

We then did some lateral-directional work. I slowed the Learjet to 170 knots for this because of sideslip limitations. We started with the baseline aircraft. An application of right rudder with positive dihedral set up on the VSS initiated a left sideslip and the left wing rose in a conventional manner. Just like a normal airplane. Positive dihedral tended to level the wings if the aircraft was disturbed by a gust. Nothing abnormal to report so far.

More button punching. With zero dihedral the wings stayed level throughout the sideslip. This felt strange. There was no sense of stability in roll. Then with negative dihedral set up, application of right rudder caused the left wing to drop. This resulted in an uncomfortable motion. I had never experienced this in flight before, having only seen it in textbooks on stability and control.

It was an undesirable and potentially unsafe phenomenon. Something to be avoided.

At Baker's bidding I put the tape cross on a distant cloud. Then I initiated Dutch Rolls at 170 knots by inputting a double rudder kick on the rudder pedals. The basic Dutch roll behaviour caused the cross to move in an ellipse against the cloud, as the basic yawing motion was accompanied by a rolling motion as each wing dropped in turn. After a couple of oscillations the motion died away. I had seen this characteristic on many tactical fighters. It looked conventional enough so far.

Jim Baker varied the parameters as he had done with the longitudinal motion, challenging me to identify what parameters he was varying. Correctly assessing the situation for the first couple of changes, I was caught out the third time. As I kicked left, then right rudder, the nose swung. We yawed to the left, then the right. Then instead of damping out, the nose wandered off to the left again, hesitated and then came back.

'What have I done?' asked Baker innocently. 'Decreased the damping?' I said tentatively. Baker grinned. 'Sure, the damping has changed. But you are now flying an aircraft with negative directional stability. The damping has decreased, but as a by-product of the instability.'

In my previous experience with tactical fighters, I had met up with this phenomenon, but only at supersonic speeds. It meant that the vertical fin was not big enough to restrain the sideslip. Many years previously, Chuck Yeager had barely escaped with his life in the rocket-powered Bell X-1 when negative directional stability at supersonic speeds had caused the aircraft to go out of control. Here it was, demonstrated at low speed in a normally stable jet. A humbling experience.

We were still wallowing on through the sky in a persistent Dutch roll, albeit a very untidy manoeuvre.

'Try applying a bit of sideslip,' said Jim Baker. I lightly pressed on the right rudder pedal. The nose lurched to the right, with the sideslip needle on the panel oscillating between six and eight degrees. It was very uncomfortable. We seemed to be flying sideways and the lateral g-force was pushing me into the corner of my seat. In a way, it was like flying the Pitts, where the minuscule vertical fin gave marginal stability but enabled it to have unparalleled agility.

With fuel now down to 2,000lb, we had completed our schedule. I brought the Learjet back to Edwards, descending to follow an F-15E on an approach over the lakebed. Jim Baker disengaged the VSS and took over for a landing on Runway 22 after just over two hours airborne. The wind had increased and was gusting to thirty-five knots, with the wind buffeting the aircraft during the lengthy taxi crosswind back to the ramp. We were guided efficiently into our parking slot and Baker shut down the engines.

As the engines whined into silence, I reflected that this Learjet provided an efficient platform for assessing the handling qualities of a range of aircraft, even to the extent of safely demonstrating some characteristics which would be too dangerous to be demonstrated in a fixed stability aircraft.

The capability was awesome, giving the pilot the ability to fly maybe twenty different aircraft within a single sortie. An invaluable tool for this task of teaching test pilots. All aircraft designers should have access to such an aircraft before finalising their designs.

Every pilot should have one.

24

Free as a Bird

As I pulled the cable release knob there was a bang and the tow cable snaked away, dragging with it the noise of the straining L-19 pulling me up to altitude. I trimmed out the sailplane, letting the airspeed drift down to the forty-two knots which would give me maximum efficiency. Happy with the speed I fussed with the rudder pedals to get the yaw string streaming centrally back over the windshield in front of me. Foolproof and cheap, the string reacted to any change in airstream direction and was a good indication of whether I had been inadvertently flying with sideslip.

It was a weekend in southern California and here I was comfortably reclining under the bubble canopy of the Grob sailplane. As the towplane dived away, it was very quiet in the cockpit, with only the soft hiss of the wind rushing past the Plexiglass to mark my progress through the air.

Slowly as I became attuned to this machine again, I became aware of a familiar feeling. Unsure for a moment, I searched my memory. It was over twenty years since I started gliding back in England. In those days we flew rather primitive wood and fabric gliders. This sleek fibreglass ship was a world apart. So it wasn't that.

The countryside below was still an alien and parched landscape, punctuated with Joshua trees, upraised arms frozen in supplication. The neat English fields, green with the perennial rains and bordered with hedgerows, were half a world away from this. Then it crept up on me. I recognised the strange sensation. It was a case of *déjà vu*. Although this cockpit was lacking the usual plethora of avionics, the sensation was not unlike that of flying a modern jet fighter. The smoothness of flight, the lack of vibration and the barely sensed sound. All the same.

But here the similarity ended. Here there was no sense of urgent motion, no watching the fuel needles sinking inexorably towards EMPTY as a thirsty jet engine gobbled up kerosene. I was not streaking across the sky, outrunning the noise. On the contrary, I was suspended over the Mojave desert, sitting comfortably in my sheepskin-lined seat, almost stationary, heading into a natural bowl on the north side of the San Gabriel mountains.

The source of power keeping the sailplane aloft was simply the sun shining benignly down from a winter sky in California. A few degrees of temperature difference between the desert floor and the wooded slopes of the bowl was enough to trigger a thermal, a bubble of warmer air which would break

The Ultimate High. The author preparing to take to the skies in the Pitts S 2A, being assisted by his children, Suzanne and Simon. *(Clare Brown)*

The de Havilland Chipmunk was a delightful trainer which was still used by the Royal Air Force in the eighties. No.10 Air Experience Flight operated these Chipmunks from RAF Woodvale. *(David Brown)*

Production flight testing on the Jet Provost Mk5 was a return to the pre-computer age of flight testing. A stopwatch and kneepad were still the tools of the trade for the flight test crew. *(British Aerospace)*

Tiger Moth G-ALNA was a classic biplane tourer well suited to flying on a British summer's day. *(David Brown)*

The Jaguar, a joint French–British project, required a hectic flight test programme which involved regular commuting by air between the respective flight test centres at Warton, in the north of England, and Istres, in the south of France. Prototype XW 563 is shown here during trials near Warton where it landed on a stretch of motorway under construction. The Jaguar was then loaded with bombs under the shelter of a road bridge, and is pictured during the subsequent take-off. *(AeroPix International)*

The swing-wing Tornado introduced a new series of challenges during the seventies. Ever-increasing masses of data were generated on each test flight. During the seventies this tri-national programme broke new ground in the highly complex world of flight testing. *(British Aerospace)*

In at the deep end. Flying a J-3 Cub at the Salton Sea was a new piloting experience. *(David Brown)*

Test Pilot for a Day. The supersonic Northrop T-38 was the mainstay of the USAF Training Command advanced training fleet from the fifties to the present day. The author found out what was involved in the making of a test pilot when he flew a T-38 with the USAF Test Pilot School at Edwards AFB. *(AeroPix International)*

Warbird Restoration. John Collver's beautifully restored SNJ-5 was a delight to fly. *(David Brown)*

Heinemann's Hot Rod. The diminutive A-4 was still operated by the Marine Corps and the US Navy into the eighties. Superb handling made it well suited for Forward Air Control duties. The author (R) with Lt Col Schriber after flying a FAC mission. *(AeroPix International)*

Night Owl. The OV-10D had an infra-red sensor and laser in the chin-mounted turret which enabled it to engage targets on the darkest of nights. *(AeroPix International)*

Riding the friendly giant. Trying to fly Goodyear's Blimp *Columbia* was an experience more akin to persuading a grazing elephant to move in the right direction. *(AeroPix International)*

Wild Weasel. Bristling with antennae for their APR-38 electronics, the
F-4G Phantoms of the Wild Weasel Units detected the emissions from
hostile radars. Anti-radar HARM missiles homed in on the radars and
destroyed them. *(AeroPix International)*

The Time Machine. This red and white Learjet, operated by Calspan, was
equipped with a variable stability flight control system. This gave it the
capability to simulate the flight behaviour of a large variety of aircraft,
including quirks and idiosyncrasies. It proved an invaluable tool to the
aircraft designer or the student test pilot at the USAF or USN Test Pilot
Schools. *(Calspan)*

The author in the cockpit of the F-15 – the largest and most powerful fighter operated by the US Air Force. *(AeroPix International)*

View from the cockpit. An F-4 Phantom over the snow-covered Sierras. *(AeroPix International)*

free from the ground and ascend invisibly into the sky. If I could intercept the thermal, the rising air would be enough to keep me airborne. This sleek fibreglass Grob still amazed me with its performance as I drifted slowly towards the bowl, barely losing altitude.

Two miles behind the tail of the Grob lay the tiny airport at Pearblossom, east of Palmdale. The small hut containing the Flying Club at Pearblossom had a record of recent flights affixed to the wall. Sailplane flights made from the field had ended in such faraway places as Cedar City, Utah, Las Vegas, Nevada and Bishop in northern California.

These were destinations I normally would consider worthy of a respectable cross-country flight in a power plane. I would achieve nothing like that on this flight. So far I had not found any lift. The sky was an unrelenting blue, with none of the haziness caused by rising air or even a wisp of forming cloud topping a thermal. Inexorably the altimeter started creeping backwards round the dial. Disappointed, I headed back towards the field, checking for other traffic and curving round into the pattern. Airbrakes out, the Grob slid down final approach, quickly losing altitude until the wheel rumbled on the runway.

Later in the afternoon I tried again. Others who had launched later had managed to stay aloft, circling like a swarm of white butterflies in weak thermals away from the field. No record trips today, but I would try again. Checking the ship again, I wheeled it into position, climbed in and carefully tightened my straps. The L-19 whooshed past me as the tow-plane landed and settled onto the runway, swiftly turning with a burst of power to taxi back. A crewman raised my wingtip. I carried out my checks and finally was hooked up to the tow plane.

Ready to go, I waggled the rudder as a visual signal to the tow-plane pilot. A blast of exhaust fumes wafted past from the L-19, percolating through the air vents. The cable tightened and we accelerated away, the wheel inches below my seat rumbling over the gravel runway. The controls came to life as the airspeed increased and the Grob lifted off before the tow-plane. For the moment I concentrated on keeping station, maintaining the wing of the L-19 just on the horizon as he spiralled up to altitude.

My spirits rose again as my horizons expanded. Away to the north the jagged skyline of the Sierra Nevada marched into the distance, with the white frieze of the first snows of winter matched by the white brilliance of the salt flats at Muroc Dry Lake at the foot of the mountains. At 3,000 feet above the high desert I pulled the release. Once free of the tow cable, the Grob lost speed. The other instruments seemed locked into place. The sailplane with its 35:1 glide ratio did not perceptibly lose height for some time.

I was looking for lift. No thermals at first, then I decided to try nearer the slope. Easing the stick and rudder over to the right, I let the sailplane sidle closer to the wooded slope. The VSI quivered to give a positive climb for a moment and the right wing twitched upwards. I started turning, managing to stick with the thermal for half a turn before sliding out of the lift.

Making another lazy circle, I hit the lift again and this time managed to centre in the thermal. The VSI bounced up to show an intermittent climb and eventually the altimeter showed a slow increase. Careful now. Don't stall in the turn. I pushed the rudder pedal, eased back on the stick, backed off on the ailerons and kept turning. The inertia of the long wings and the relatively ineffective ailerons made it hard work to keep in the thermal. I worked the lift for a couple of hundred feet before it petered out. Just enough altitude to turn out of the bowl and head north, over a ridge and back towards the field.

The Grob loitered along, trimmed at its best glide of forty-two knots as I hunted for thermals. When I started flying out here in the Mojave, to my unpractised eye one spot of desert looked very much like another, but my instructor, Ed Green, knew the countryside around the field like the back of his hand. Whereas I saw only unpaved tracks and areas of rocky ground, he saw each one as a possible thermal source even this late in the year.

Now I hunted for thermals. After another tussle with an embryo thermal I ran out of altitude and start setting up for an approach to the west, into the light breeze. But no. The windsock showed that the wind had switched round and was now coming from the east. The start of a Santa Ana wind, perhaps? I could see the tow-planes moving about on the ground, setting up to launch from the western end of the field. So I turned overhead the field and set up for an approach for a landing to the east.

This is where the good visibility from the bubble canopy was a boon. Sailplanes spend a lot of their time turning, often in close proximity to others sharing the same lift. As the Grob arced round at the end of the downwind leg I let the speed drift up to guard against wind shear. My idle left hand finally eased back on the airbrake lever and the rate of descent increased. Over the runway now and I flared, a fraction high as I forgot just how low the Grob was to the ground, and eased it down until I heard the single wheel rumble. Speedbrakes now came fully out to slow the forward rush, and I pulled the lever to the rearmost position, so actuating the wheel brake. In a minor victory, I judged it correctly and the Grob coasted to a halt next to the waiting tow-plane.

The change of wind might do the trick. I was eternally optimistic. My father, fishing back in England, would always know that the next cast would connect him with the biggest fish in the river. Similarly, I knew that there was a thermal out there, just waiting for me.

One more launch. Five minutes later I pulled the release and the tan-coloured L-19 banked, dropping out of my world. Once off tow I eased closer to the hillside and succeeded in finding some lift coming off the rocks.

FREE AS A BIRD

Wheeling and soaring over the wooded crags in these foothills of the San Gabriels, I lifted the Grob easily over ridges in an exhilarating ride before gliding silently back out over the desert again. The air trembled under my wings. I looked over the side. A park crammed with recreational vehicles lay below. Maybe there was some activity there. I turned a full circle over the tiny oblong shapes of the RVs, but the air remained smooth. I had lost the thermal. I tried the bend of the dry river bed . . . nothing. The altimeter was creeping downwards and I was still some miles away from the field.

It was too late in the day for thermals. I admitted it to myself as I whispered back to the field. Less than two miles from the field, with a few hundred feet of precious altitude to play with, I decided to stall the Grob in straight and level flight. It was some time since I had practised this. Stalls were fun. As I eased the stick back the airspeed needle wavered off the bottom end of the scale. It got very quiet as the airspeed bled away. Under my hand the stick grew sloppy as the controls ran out of air. Eventually the nose fell away as the wing quit flying. The Grob was just another flying machine after all and I gained airspeed by lowering the nose although I found my left hand trying to push an imaginary throttle forward.

With the field below, I drifted down to my last landing of the day.

As the sun set I drove home down the crowded freeway, tired from the concentration, but very satisfied even though the day had produced no spectacular results. No climbs to stratospheric altitudes. The Sierra Wave would have to wait for another day.

Almost daily I enviously watched kestrels and red-tailed hawks circling effortlessly over grassland behind our house. Sailplaning was the nearest I could get to that condition. It was a challenging aspect of flying. Free as a bird . . . just that we humans had to work harder.

25

Eagle Country

Daylight came grudgingly to the winter desert, then suddenly the first rays of the sun cast a blinding reflection from the salt of the dry lake bed. I screwed my eyes up against the glare, squinting at the hulking silhouette of the fighter looming before me on the ramp.

That January day at Edwards Air Force Base marked my initiation into the world of the supersonic fighter. The United States operated three of these: the F-15, F-16 and F/A-18. It was rare for a non-military pilot to fly one of these potent machines.

During a visit to Edwards to write about the F-15 Combined Test Force, I had been offered the rare opportunity of flying in the F-15. Arguably the best air superiority fighter of the seventies and early eighties, the F-15 was a large aircraft, powered by two Pratt & Whitney F-100 engines which gave it a thrust-to-weight ratio of greater than one, so enabling the aircraft to accelerate vertically upwards at light weight. I had first seen the awesome performance of the brightly painted F-15B in bicentennial red, white and blue colours at Farnborough back in 1976. It was a long-felt wish of mine to see how this aircraft performed.

The usual walk-round confirmed the awesome size of this grey-painted fighter, its delta wing high enough to walk under with ease and the gaping box-like structures of the sophisticated all-moving air inlets flanking the cockpit. As if to confirm the lethal mission of the Eagle, I could see, inset into the wing, the muzzle for the M-61 cannon.

The twin tails of the F-15B, flanking the huge afterburner nozzles of the engines, were emblazoned with the IFFC badge. This acronym stood for Integrated Fire/Flight Controls system which could couple the flight controls and armament system together. In a series of trials prior to my flight this aircraft had wrung out the system, with live gun firings culminating in the spectacular destruction of a manoeuvring F-102 drone fighter.

Flying the Eagle on this mission was Squadron Leader Rick Pope, RAF, a test pilot on an exchange posting with the USAF. Our mission objective was simple: to look at the handling and performance of this fighter throughout the envelope.

Just after dawn, it was still below freezing as I carefully climbed the ladder to the F-15's rear cockpit. My caution was well-founded, as I could see a veneer of ice on the top of the inlet.

I strapped in while Rick Pope finished pre-flighting the aircraft and then climbed the ladder to the front cockpit. Getting ready for business I checked that my g-suit was plugged in, oxygen was switched on and my helmet and mask were adjusted. Reviewing my briefing notes I reminded myself that the limits on the aircraft were thirty units of angle of attack (AoA) and Mach 1.5/660 knots, respectable limits even with our 600-gallon centreline external tank. All the numbers were big with this aircraft. Fuel capacity was a couple of orders of magnitude larger than my little aerobatic aircraft. We had 15,200lb of fuel on board, with 11,200lb in the internal tanks plus the 4,000lb in the centreline tank. A lot of fuel for a lot of aircraft.

At take-off the Eagle would weigh over twenty tons.

The Eagle had a roomy cockpit. Flight instruments were spread out on the panel in front of me with engine gauges off to the right. Two grey-painted consoles flanked the cockpit, crammed with systems controls and switches. The two hefty throttles were under my left hand. Just above my left knee on the panel was the electronic navigation display, surrounded by a multiplicity of mode buttons. This panel also held the radar display and my HUD repeater.

By now we were ready to go and the Jet Fuel Starter (JFS) wailed into life. Once the JFS was running, Rick Pope started the right engine. As the big engine wound up, the needles on the engine gauges began marching round their dials. Once the engine lit with a rumble the exhaust gas temperature shot up, then slowed as the engine settled at fifty-five per cent at ground idle. While I was head-down in the cockpit, familiarising myself with the NAV display, suddenly the right hand inlet slammed down, banging against the stops and then eerily going through its own automatic sequence of pre-flight checks. Despite the momentary jump in my heart rate, all this was normal. In fact Rick Pope had warned me of the inlet behaviour during our briefing. I was now thoroughly awake as the left engine started winding up and in turn the left inlet clanged down. With electrical power now available, I motored the ejection seat down to its lowest position, primarily to get out of the still freezing air while Pope carried out more control checks. This F-15 had a non-standard digital flight control system and we would be assessing it during our flight.

These big engines were thirsty. Just sitting in the chocks we were burning 700 pounds per hour on each engine at idle. I quickly reviewed my checklist for my impending role in setting up the navigation system, a necessary step before we could fly. If it did not work the first time we would be forced to recycle the system to retrieve the situation.

The latitude and longitude of our exact position on the ramp had been inserted into the computer the previous night. It was time for me to set my NAV control panel rotary switch to GND ALIGN. When I got the expected mode indications on the NAV display, following my checklist I pushed the third (NAV) button down on the NAV display and breathed a sigh of relief as the computer accepted the information and the ALIGN TIME counter (ATIME) started to count up from zero. It could take five minutes – three hundred seconds – for the system to align. Until then we could not move the aircraft and while I monitored the counter we completed our radio checks and listened to ATIS, the recorded tower information. Unemotionally ATIS informed us that the air temperature was still below freezing, thirty degrees Fahrenheit. I shivered. It felt cold.

'Arms in?' Pope sang out and I made sure everything was clear of the canopy. There was a sigh of hydraulics as the canopy came down and slid forward an inch or two to lock with a solid clunk. As the seal inflated the canopy warning light extinguished and I felt the pressure build up on my ears. Pope finished off the control checks, continuing a dialogue with our crew chief on the ramp who was patched into the intercom. Speedbrake and flaps were cycled. Everything checked out OK and at last the cockpit was warming up.

After what seemed like an eternity, ATIME counted up through 300 seconds. I informed my pilot, then switched to NAV mode. From that moment, our inertial system would monitor our movements in space, and continuously update our position. Brakes were released, the throttles were eased forward and we taxied forward a couple of feet. The nose of the Eagle nodded as the brakes were checked and we started the long taxi out to the head of the runway.

Appropriately in its role as the main landing base for the Shuttle Orbiter, Edwards AFB now had a new and futuristic concrete pinnacle for a control tower, replacing its old red-painted corrugated iron predecessor. Once we had rolled past the tower, Pope swung us off to the left near the head of the runway. We stopped in the run-up area. While we kept our hands on our helmets, away from any controls, ground personnel scurried underneath, checking for leaks or loose panels.

Despite the early hour we found ourselves in line behind the morning contingent of test aircraft from the Test Pilot School. As we waited, one all-white T-38 of the TPS developed a snag. The jet shut down and the disgruntled crew climbed out. I crossed my fingers. But a minute later we were given a thumbs up and were moved on our way.

The controller cleared us onto the runway. This was the main shuttle landing runway, over two miles long, plenty long enough for us today. Rick Pope ran the engines up to eighty per cent against the brakes. It was noisy and the nose dipped under the thrust of the engines.

'This will be an afterburner take-off,' Pope's voice reminded me; 'We'll rotate at 120 knots and will be off the ground at 155.'

The engines were stabilised at eighty per cent, the highest that could be held on the brakes. My pulse rate was a little higher than normal. Pope released the brakes. I punched my stopwatch as we started to move, passing the big '14' marker sign at the side of the runway, signifying 14,000 feet of runway in front of us. Out of the corner of my eye I saw the throttles go forward to military power and then smoothly go through into the after-burner range. There was an increasing push in my back and a rumble from somewhere behind me. The nose wavered a hair to the left, then recovered. 'Left's a touch slow to light,' commented Pope, then we were accelerating powerfully, both nozzles fully open and 23,000lb of thrust from each F-100 giving that inexorable shove in the back.

The next marker board – '13' – was by now hurtling towards us and my stopwatch was still reading under ten seconds when we rotated and floated off the ground. There was a flash of a red warning light down to my left knee as the gear started to retract. The gear locked up, we came out of afterburner and there was a heavy vibration from the nosewheel, retracting virtually under my seat and still spinning. As the vibration died away we were acceler-ating through 250 knots. In military power the cockpit was momentarily quiet. Seconds later, as our Eagle flashed over the field boundary, we were cleared to climb to altitude.

This promised to be interesting. On numerous occasions I had watched F-15s flying out of the McDonnell factory at St Louis. Scorning the more pedestrian airliner departure profiles, the Eagles invariably performed spec-tacular VIKING departures, roaring almost vertically upwards until lost to sight. Now it was my turn to sample this experience.

'Burners going in now.'

As the burners lit we rotated nose up to about seventy degrees and that awesome acceleration kept pushing. I unlocked my shoulder harness and twisted round to see the ground dropping away at an impressive rate between the twin tails. Eyes front again, with my eyes drawn hypnotically to the alti-meter. The needle was spinning round as if demented while the drum counter was already indicating that we were nearing 20,000 feet in less than a minute. We were still climbing like a rocket, almost vertically, when Rick Pope rolled us inverted, pulling down to the horizon as we came out of after-burner.

I remembered to breathe again.

We rolled out, level at 25,000 feet and heading north. Pope handed control of the jet over to me. Still mentally trying to catch up, and very aware of the sheer size of this machine, I wiggled the stick, expecting to have to use a lot of muscle on the controls. I was wrong. With the Eagle's fully powered hydraulic controls, a little effort went a long way. The ailerons seemed to have a mind of their own and I over-corrected at first, setting up a small-

135

amplitude oscillation as the horizon rocked gently from side to side. It took a few seconds to get the hang of it. Once I was holding the stick lightly between finger and thumb, the aircraft went back to flying smoothly. It was time to relax and look at the view.

It was a beautiful cloudless morning over the ochre sandy wastes of the Mojave Desert. The rising sun behind us was casting long shadows on the desert below. Our flight plan would take the F-15 round the Blue Route, one of the low-level routes used day and night by the CTF for systems testing and for the Lantirn testing on the F-15E. Following the low-level mission, we would look at the aircraft handling with the digital control system.

Visibility from the bubble canopy was superb. Sliding into view to the left of the nose, some five miles below, was a circular tank on the ground. This was our Initial Point for entrance to the circuitous Blue Route. As California City slid past below on my left, it was time to descend. I pushed over, banked to the right and started descending to the start of the Blue Route. We whispered down, down, down, paralleling a rocky spine of hills rising to our left. Flying with my right hand, I took my left hand off the throttles and blipped the switch to raise my seat upwards, craning to look past the headrest of the front seat.

We whispered down to 500 feet above the rocky slopes. Easing the throttles forward, we stabilised around 350 knots. I settled down to the unaccustomed feeling of low flying the large aircraft in this environment. At that moment my HUD repeater decided to quit, so robbing me of my primary navigational aid. So I was basically left to navigate the hard way, with a map, compass and stopwatch. No sympathy from Pope, who, as he pointed out, used to do the same thing when flying Hunters in the RAF. Consequently I was kept working hard as our turnpoints and landmarks came up very quickly.

The exceptional visibility helped. In all directions we could see out to the saw-toothed horizon. Over to our left sprawled the Naval Weapons Center at China Lake. There were buildings ahead, so we climbed to 1,500 feet over Searles lakebed, weirdly patterned with salt evaporators, and streaked over a steam-belching industrial complex. Passing the airfield at Trona I was cleared to descend again, heading for a saddle in the hills that would take us into Panamint Valley.

As the Eagle overflew the ridge, there was a jolt from air turbulence. The big wing, designed primarily for a turning dogfight, did not take kindly to turbulence. Now the valley floor was falling away beneath us, although off our starboard wing Sentinel Peak jutted two miles into the sky. Further east lay Death Valley which in parts was below sea level. We pressed on into Panamint Valley and our target at Ballarat radar station.

Pope took over for some serious low level flying. Almost alongside my cockpit I could see our shadow speeding over the scrub-covered wastes. Low down over the desert, my view was restricted to a kaleidoscope of impressions: scrub . . . rocks . . . vehicle tracks . . . all blurred past. We flashed overhead the radar station at Ballarat, its antennae rotating.

Still accelerating, airspeed was now up to 500 knots as we made our escape from the imaginary ground defences. Pope, a former Tornado test pilot at Bedford, was at home at these low levels. I could see, over his helmet, at the end of the valley a rocky knoll jutting skywards which marked our next turn point.

There was a tremendous impression of speed. This low down, we would be almost invulnerable from interception. Our escape assured, we pulled round the knoll. Pope handed control back to me. Easing the stick back and the throttles forward, I flew westwards up the steep slope of the mountain until in seconds we crested the ridgeline at 10,000 feet and sailed out into space. The sight was awesome. Below us was spread the expanse of Owens Lake with the spectacular snow-covered range of Sierras barring our way from horizon to horizon.

The cockpit was quiet as we threaded our way into the Sierras, following the valleys as we climbed, with the great rock pile of Mount Whitney jutting skywards off to our right. Occasionally an ice-covered road wound its way up a valley and we passed over frozen lakes covered in drifting snow. It looked unbearably desolate. We had dressed warmly for this flight, in the eventuality of having to walk out, but I gave an involuntary shiver. In this frozen landscape the only colour was on the sides of Mount Whitney, where large sheets of vertical yellowish-grey rock were revealed where the snow had lost its frigid grip on the rock faces.

Following the map, I turned south and headed towards Lake Isabella. More confident now, I was getting used to the big fighter, letting down over a thickly wooded valley on our route. A frozen stream slid past below as I eased lower, heading for a notch in the mountains which would take us into the next valley. A glance at the altimeter revealed that we were flying at just over eleven thousand feet. It was a strange feeling, being this close to the ground when over two miles high. By now I was peering intently past the front seat, aiming for the notch. As we sped through the notch the trees whipped past on either side.

I said thoughtfully to Pope: '. . . and you do this at *night* during the Lantirn flying?'

'Yes,' came the casual rejoinder. 'The worst bit is when the rotating beacon is illuminating the trees on either side . . .'

Before I could ponder too much on this statement, I was pulling hard round a turn in the valley only to come across an innocuous bank of cloud filling the valley and blanketing our path. Obviously that finished low flying for us today on the Blue Route and I pulled up out of the valley, eased the throttles forward to military power and climbed away.

We still had sufficient fuel and time to look at the handling of this air superiority fighter in its natural element. Aerobatics in such a powerful aircraft promised to be exciting. We levelled at fifteen thousand feet over a snow-white rumpled cloud deck, alone in a brilliant bowl of cerulean blue.

I started with a loop. Even with the throttles at military power in level flight the F-15 was accelerating through 380 knots within seconds. A slight backward pressure started the nose rising. I continued the pull, slackening off slightly as we floated inverted at the top of the loop at 20,000 feet. Easing back on the throttles, we started plummeting towards the cloud deck. I pulled harder; the Eagle was up to twenty-five units angle of attack and the whole aircraft was buffeting. The g-suit squeezed hard and I was forced down into the seat until I unloaded into level flight.

At this point Rick Pope said, 'To make things interesting, I'll show you a 250 knot loop.' Setting up the aircraft at 250 knots, he selected both engines into afterburner and pulled hard on the stick. Trailing flame and thunder, the F-15 stood on its tail and gracefully arced up into the blue, with the angle of attack indicator wavering almost at our thirty unit limit. With the thrust just balancing the high induced drag of the big wing, we were inverted a mere 4,500 feet above our starting altitude. Then down the other side and we completed the loop with the airspeed still at 250 knots, some 300 feet higher than we started. It was an amazing demonstration of the tractability of this big fighter.

I tried a few rolls. Aileron rolls were no sweat and the roll rate was impressive even with partial stick deflection. I then got a little over-enthusiastic and performed a four-point hesitation roll which involved some pretty hefty roll accelerations. As we reached the inverted point Pope's map book of the Blue Route was torn from its Velcro stowage, sailed out of the forward cockpit, pirouetted between us, bounced off the canopy, then floated into my cockpit where I grabbed it as we came upright again.

How was the turning performance of the Eagle? Impressive. Turns at military power with only a moderate single-handed pull force, pursuing an imaginary MiG, resulted in high sustained turn rates with my g-suit squeezing hard.

I had long promised myself a look at the Eagle's low speed handling. Having flown in the F-4 with the Wild Weasels, I knew that the F-4 had low-speed handling problems. Hard manoeuvring at low speed could result in a departure from controlled flight, a manoeuvre known as 'The Thing' to former Vietnam-era F-4 jockeys. In contrast to the automatic flaps and slats on the later generation F-16 and F/A-18, the Eagle had nothing more than a big cambered delta wing bereft of sophisticated high-lift devices. So I

138

pulled back on the throttles and we started to slow down. Sailing out over the edge of the cloud deck we headed out over the rust-coloured palette of the Mojave Desert and towards the white glare of Cuddeback Dry Lake.

To lose more speed, I pulled back on the slide button on the right throttle and the speedbrake popped out from the top of the fuselage behind the canopy. I could see the speedbrake, visible in my rear view mirror on the windscreen arch. As speed dropped off to 150 knots, I retracted the speed-brake and nudged the throttles up to stabilise the speed.

At this low speed, although we were in buffet, I still had full aileron control. I banked left, then right and the Eagle responded without fuss. Rick Pope then took over, manoeuvring more positively and using rudder to point the nose at an imaginary target, finally completing a full aileron roll with the ASI hovering around 150 knots throughout.

The whole sequence was made more impressive by its lack of drama. 'By now,' said Rick Pope drily, 'an F-4 would be spinning.'

It was time to go back. We continued descending, past the Boron mines and on to the ILS for Edwards. With gear and flaps down, our flight path crossed Rogers Dry Lake and suddenly we were in the middle of a crowded traffic pattern, with an F-4, a T-38 and another F-15 all competing for slots in the pattern. Pope let me continue the approach and I drove my seat up to peer over the nose.

Meanwhile on the lakebed below another F-4 had landed, dragging a trail of salt, pursued by the crash trucks. The lakebed at Edwards was used almost every day for precautionary landings. This incident was not regarded as any-thing unusual and having the option to use the lakebed made life much simpler for an aircraft with hydraulic or brake problems.

Close-in now, I saw that the F-4 and the F-15 were both down on the runway, so we overshot in military power, cleaning up and pulling hard left over the south base to the downwind leg for a touch-and-go.

Downwind, we nailed the altitude and pulled back the throttles to slow below gear limit speed of 250 knots. There was a blast from the audio warning, as we lost speed with the gear still up and the engines were spooled up until the warning tone stopped. The gear and flaps went down. I needed another four per cent rpm to counter the drag and a touch of nose-down trim as the aircraft tended to balloon upwards. The drum altimeter was locked on 3,800 feet, pattern altitude over the high desert base, as the end of the landing runway slid past our nine o'clock and we headed out over the lakebed, patterned by the weird array of lines and triangles which were cues for the shuttle pilots.

We started a descending turn, steady on 150 knots and twenty units AoA. As we curved towards the runway, the air was calm and as the runway van-ished under the nose the wings were rolled level and the stick eased back.

The big wing took over in ground effect and we floated for a second until a rumble signified that we were down. An exceptionally smooth landing. With the throttles pushed up to the military power throttle stop the Eagle got smartly airborne again.

Once more around the pattern, and down again for a full stop landing. Standard practice for a full stop landing in the F-15 was to keep the nose up to thirteen degrees for aero braking above ninety knots to save burning out the brakes. Fifteen degrees of pitch would scrape the tail. Pope kept the nose up as the speed bled off. The nose eventually dropped and we slowed, then exited the runway. During the long taxi back I began to realise just what a tremendous jump in performance had been achieved in this generation of fighters.

Back at the CTF we parked among the dark F-15Es and the lighter F-15A fighters being readied for the day's flight test schedule.

As the engines whined down into silence and we unstrapped, I had to agree that the Eagle was indeed a mighty machine.

26
Electric Jet

At 40,000 feet the sky was impossibly blue as the F-16B headed south over the Mojave Desert. The view from under the bubble canopy was awesome. We were arrowing southwards, a snow-white condensation trail marking our pathway across the sky. Off to our right the snow-capped Sierra Nevada marked the backbone of California. In front lay the expanse of the Mojave Desert, backed by the San Gabriel mountains. Nearer to hand, dotted about the desert, lay the dry lakebeds used as emergency landing sites back in the rocket flying days.

Close below were Cuddeback and Harper Dry Lakes. Further away lay Rosamund and the expanse of Rogers Dry Lake, bordered by the cluster of tiny dots which were the huge hangars at Edwards AFB, from where we had taken off less than an hour ago.

In the front seat of the diminutive fighter was John Fergione, Chief of Flight Operations at Edwards AFB for General Dynamics, builders of the F-16. Now, with the throttle eased forward to the military power detent, we were accelerating. It was still quiet in the cockpit and uncannily smooth. Cabin altitude was 15,000 feet and the doll's eye of my oxygen flow indicator blinked rhythmically in time with my breathing. The ejection seat in the F-16 was reclined thirty degrees. Primarily designed that way to increase the g-tolerance of the pilot, the result was a very relaxing posture, unlike the seats in certain other jets I had flown.

At Mach .86 there was a barely perceptible shudder as the airflow started to go supersonic over our wings. We watched our Machmeters creep upwards. At Mach .98 my Machmeter needle hesitated as the airflow piling up in front of the aircraft increased the drag. Fergione eased the nose down a fraction. We continued to watch the instruments intently. At 39,000 feet and Mach .95 the altimeter needle quivered, swung crazily and settled down again as the shockwave eased back over the static ports. Simultaneously the Machmeter swung up to Mach 1.05. It was an event marked only by its lack of drama.

We were supersonic, still in dry power and the F-16 was not even breathing hard. If the throttle was fully foward, at the full afterburner position, the F-16 could zip out to better than Mach 2.0 but naturally would gulp fuel at a horrendous rate in the process.

I could not help thinking that it was a mere forty years since Chuck Yeager had gone supersonic for the first time in the Bell X-1 in this very same patch of sky. In those days it needed a B-29 mother ship, chase planes, rocket power and a big step into the unknown to accomplish supersonic flight. We had just done it in a routine manner.

We continued descending, accelerating to Mach 1.2 as we neared the lower edge of our reserved airspace. Fergione throttled back into subsonic flight for me to fly the aircraft through a few manoeuvres. By now our double boom from the shockwaves was heading off towards Edwards to rattle the windows and the hangar doors, just as similar sonic booms had cracked across the field periodically throughout the day.

Another assignment had sent me on this visit to the F-16 Combined Test Force at Edwards. Operated, as the title implied, by a mix of USAF and contractor personnel, the CTF had given me an opportunity to fly on a mission which would take us through the low-level route north of Edwards before climbing up to the supersonic corridor for a brief look at supersonic flight. Then I would be given an opportunity to look at the handling of the F-16. This was the newest fighter operated by the US Air Force. It was a rare privilege to fly this fighter.

After being fitted out with flight gear in the flight equipment section, we had walked out to our F-16B parked on the bustling flightline outside the CTF. The flightline was crowded with single- and two-seat F-16s. Some F-16s were involved with testing of Lantirn pods on low-level night missions. Another F-16, spin chute cantilevered out behind the tail, was busy with high angle of attack investigations. Others were scheduled for performance testing with the new F-110 engine.

Our callsign was ZOOM 76. While John Fergione pre-flighted the ship I climbed the ladder and slid into the rear cockpit. Pushing my feet forward in the tunnels, I connected up the sidestraps, lap strap and chest strap linking me to the ACES 2 ejection seat. I checked that the vitally important g-suit was plugged in. As I donned my helmet and mask, Fergione climbed into the front seat. Leaning forward I adjusted my rudder pedals and got ready for business.

The canopy, a single-piece three-quarters of an inch thick monolithic polycarbonate transparency, sighed down and locked. On the F-16 the conventional windscreen and canopy were combined into this single unit. The resulting visibility was superb, with none of the usual obstructions from the canopy bow found on earlier fighters. There was a price to pay. Fergione had briefed that if we had to eject, I would go first, and would automatically eject the canopy, myself and Fergione in that order. I resolved not to eject unless things really looked serious.

Our Jet Fuel Starter (JFS) whined into life. At twenty-five per cent rpm the engine lit up with a rumble with the generator coming on line a few seconds later. While we checked our caution lights around the cockpits the Inertial Navigation System (INS) was aligning. The INS held up to ten waypoints, gave our present position, presented steering information on the Head Up Display (HUD) and also calculated the wind speed and direction. It was certainly better than following railroad tracks.

The F-16 was an unstable fly-by-wire aircraft, known as the Electric Jet by its pilots. Consequently an exhaustive flight controls automatic checkout was necessary before we could fly. It took a few minutes of teamwork between pilot and ground crew before we got confirmation that our flight controls checked out. Then over the radio Edwards Tower cleared ZOOM 76 to Amber route for the low-level portion of our mission. However we were still waiting for the INS to align.

In the rear cockpit I had a HUD repeater showing the view through the pilot's HUD overlaying a green-tinted video picture of the outside world. I fiddled with the display, adjusting the picture showing the hangar and the groundcrew walking on the ramp. By the time I was satisfied with the brightness, the INS platform was aligned and we were ready to go.

We taxied out and I checked my g-suit by pushing the button at the rear of the left hand console. The suit inflated, putting my legs and abdomen in a vice-like grip until I released the button. There was no doubt that the suit was working. With the tremendous agility of this fighter, F-16 pilots could lose consciousness if the g-suit became disconnected during hard manoeuvres.

Our groundcrew had by now piled into a van and had followed us out to the head of the runway, where they scurried about under the craft, giving us a final visual check.

ZOOM 76 was cleared onto the runway. We armed our seats. I could not help thinking of the various numbers Fergione had quoted at the briefing. We were loaded with just over 5,000lb of fuel. This put our weight at around 23,000lb. Our F-100 engine gave 25,000lb of thrust, enough to launch us vertically. This promised to be a spectacular take-off.

Brakes could not hold the F-16 above eighty per cent rpm because the anti-skid system would automatically release. So Fergione set the throttle to eighty per cent and as the engine wound up he released the brakes. Advancing the throttle to military power, the rpm swung up to 100 per cent.

'We have five stages of burner. You can feel them all,' he said conversationally, advancing the throttle smoothly into the afterburner range. The last one is the biggest.'

As we accelerated, my helmet was forced back against the headrest and there was a jolt as each of the five stages of afterburner lit-up in sequence:
. . . three

. . . four

. . . *five*

There was no mistaking that last one.

With all that thrust we were by now accelerating like an arrow from a bow. Before we had reached the first thousand-foot marker on the runway we rotated at 120 knots, with the wheels off the ground at 135 knots. The gear retracted and by the end of the 13,000ft runway we were at 450 knots. A breathtaking start to any flight.

We came out of burner and climbed towards twenty thousand feet. I took control of the aircraft and started getting used to the sidestick control of the F-16. Some time earlier I had flown the variable-stability Learjet rigged to simulate an early F-16 flight control system. That system had been actuated by force sensors alone. With no movement of the stick to give cues, I had found it difficult to fly precisely. Other pilots had complained in similar fashion.

But now, in the real F-16 the sidestick on the right hand console gave me about a quarter of an inch of movement, although primarily a force-sensing device. It was surprisingly natural. An armrest supported my forearm. Use of a sidestick certainly freed up a lot of panel space in front of the pilot. The cockpit was small but adequate, almost like the Grob sailplane, although price and performance of this aircraft were multiplied many times over that of the Grob.

I cautiously tried out gentle turns left and right, then levelled off at twenty thousand feet as we headed north-west over Mojave and Tehachapi. Soon it was time to descend. Fergione took over and we spiralled down in a 4g turn, my g-suit squeezing, to enter the south end of the Amber low-level route. At 420 knots we headed north, our clear visors down to guard against possible bird strikes. Initially we headed north over the foothills of the Sierra Nevada which rose to 8,000 feet.

The ride was smooth and the ground streamed past. Lake Isabella slid past to our right. On the HUD I was intently watching my display. A pitch ladder occupied centre screen, with speed presented on the left hand side. Our heading of 350 degrees was at the bottom of the display with altitude indicated on the right.

A circular symbol on the HUD showed the position of our next waypoint. Most importantly, at that moment, the velocity vector symbol, showing our projected flight path, was perched just over the next saw-toothed ridge. As we flew north the wooded ridges in turn flashed past just underneath us.

We reached the first waypoint, a cluster of radio towers on a ridge. The waypoint symbol slid off to the right, pointing to the next waypoint. Our right wing went down and we turned right until the symbol centred again in the HUD.

144

The ride was still smooth and we were now up to 440 knots. As we headed north the ground was rising. Signs of civilisation were restricted to the occasional dirt road. Patches of snow were visible beneath the trees. The ridges running east to west became steeper and more and more spectacular as we hurdled over each one.

Waypoint 2 was a Forestry Service observation post. I looked down to see a lonely cabin located on a beetling crag, reached by a tortuous path etched across the face of the bluff.

Looking forward again I became aware of the snow-covered bulk of Mount Whitney off to our left. The mountains were rugged up here in the Sierras. We were heading north-east when turbulence started to buffet the plane. It was a washboard type of roughness, not the usual isolated jolts of convective heating. It felt as if the wind was rising. We climbed a few hundred feet but found no relief from the hard-edged jolting.

Between two ridges off to our right, Owens Lake slid into view. Stained red and white by the minerals in the water, it had the look of a surrealistic painting. The turbulence was getting worse and I was alternately jolted hard against my straps and then back into the seat. It was difficult to breathe under these conditions.

Our flight path now led us down across the Owens Valley itself, with the sheer wall of mountains looming off our left wingtip. We could see that the weather was deteriorating to the north where a series of lenticular clouds barred the valley ahead of us. This celestial staircase climbed to maybe thirty thousand feet and was the fabled Sierra wave. The rotor system associated with the mountain wave was the cause of the turbulence. In between jolts I could not help thinking, 'If only I was in a sailplane today . . .' But today was reserved for more serious business.

We overflew our next waypoint, banking hard right, now heading east across the valley towards the opposite sheer mountain wall. As a last veil of cloud drifted back above us the turbulence was suddenly switched off. Still heading for the wall of rock, Fergione pulled back on the stick, the nose came up and the velocity vector on my display rose to hover on the mountain ridge. Climbing more than a mile in a few seconds, we crested the ridge at ten thousand feet, banked right and flashed down the barren eastern slopes into Saline Valley.

Dropping two miles in a few seconds my ears started complaining until I equalised the pressure. Levelling just over the lakebed we headed south with our shadow speeding just off to my left across the scrub-covered plain. Glaring white patches of dry lakebed flashed past and we climbed slightly to avoid a jagged outcrop of rock barring our path. Then back down to hug the lakebed, heading for our target.

It was an exhilarating ride. Operationally, this low altitude minimised exposure to enemy defences, but the unremitting concentration was very exhausting.

At the southern end of the valley this lunar landscape ended in another wall of mountains. We bored on until the rock wall was high above us, then Fergione smoothly pulled the nose up and we easily outclimbed the ground as the jagged ridges rose beneath us. Seconds later, peaking at 7,000 feet, we flashed across the desolate ridge and plunged down into Panamint Valley.

I recognised this place. This is where I flew with the Wild Weasels. I remembered the solitary road snaking across the awesome immensity of the dry plain, leading towards Death Valley across the mountains to the east. Moments after we flashed across the road a glaring white lakebed blurred beneath our nose. It was incongruously quiet in the cockpit. Then a dirt road flashed diagonally beneath us, with a plume of dust signifying a solitary vehicle. At this speed we were barely a second behind our noise. The driver might with luck have seen us in his mirror, giving him warning, before the thunderclap of sound hit him . . .

I could see the target coming up on the HUD. There . . . in a split second, my mind recorded images . . . a cluster of buildings . . . a radar dish revolving . . . parked cars around the radar station, then we were fleeing across the valley floor, trailing our banner of sound.

At the southern end of Panamint Valley, we again headed straight for the mountains, but this time Fergione pulled the nose up and kept it pointing towards the vertical. The F-16 stood on its tail and kept climbing out of the low-level corridor, aiming for 40,000 feet and the supersonic corridor.

Remembering that the F-16 was a fighter, after our supersonic run I took control of the jet while we searched for targets. Reaching forward I switched my display from HUD to RADAR mode. Our radar was sensitive enough to pick up trucks on the Antelope Valley freeway. But the screen remained blank for a moment. Suddenly the Edwards controller warned us of two aircraft heading for us. We searched with the radar, varying the elevation by a throttle-mounted switch.

There they were, two targets coming towards us, head-on but lower than our F-16. The computer-generated targets had symbols with aspect angle and speed attached. Moments later we had a visual on them, a pair of white Phantoms from the test fleet at Edwards, manoeuvring in their own block of airspace below us. We pulled round after them. In the sun and ten thousand feet higher than the Phantoms we were in a perfect position for a bounce, but reluctantly had to let them go on their way.

Letting down to 15,000 feet enabled us to look at the low-speed handling of the F-16. We slowed initially to 180 knots, then 130 knots and twenty units angle of attack. By 100 knots the nose was pointing skywards with much of the lift coming from the leading edge extensions stretching either side of the cockpit. At this flight condition we were in the hands of the flight computer. Another reason for the soubriquet of 'Electric Jet'. Above fifteen AoA the computer limited our roll rate. No matter how hard I pulled back on the side-stick, the F-16 would fly at a maximum of twenty-five AoA. Pushing the rudder pedals at this flight condition had no effect as the rudder was phased out at high AoA to prevent a spin. Fergione then demonstrated the roll control at low speed by accelerating to 150 knots, then rolling the F-16 through 360 degrees. No problems. I was impressed.

Then he handed control of the aircraft over to me.

At 350 knots I started with an aileron roll to the left. Light pressure got us rolling smoothly to the left. I reversed the pressure and the roll stopped after one complete revolution. Then I repeated the roll to the right.

The feel between rolls to left and right was noticeable, like the difference between forehand and backhand at tennis. It felt very unnatural to me at first. The F-16 flight control system was set up for full control deflection in roll with only a 17lb force. That was enough, with only wrist action available to roll the aircraft.

Progressing to four-point and eight-point rolls, I was getting used to the sidestick, although the harmony between roll and pitch took a little getting used to.

Next came a loop, pulling 4g in a huge arc and topping out at 25,000 feet. This was sheer fun and the F-16 was not even working hard. Turns were similarly easy, giving tremendous agility and the ability to reverse direction in an instant, but I slackened off on the sidestick when I saw Fergione's helmet start to slide down behind his headrest, indicating that the g was getting too high. I could have pulled to the 9g limit with a 25lb pull and the aircraft would not have complained.

We were down to our BINGO fuel of 1,200lb eastbound, so to reverse direction and head for home I pulled up into an Immelmann turn, pulling 4.5g, until the horizon floated inverted over the nose, then rolled out on a westerly heading for Edwards.

'ZOOM 76. Continue descent. We have a B 1B climbing out towards you. One o'clock at three miles,' said Edwards Tower. I let down quickly towards Edwards, getting a visual on the dark arrow-like shape of the huge bomber, already two thousand feet above us as it sailed past. We continued letting down towards Rogers Dry Lake, and I levelled at pattern altitude of some fifteen hundred feet over the high desert.

We overflew the lake, offset to the right of the runway and I entered the break at 300 knots, turning through 180 degrees on to the downwind leg. Fergione took over for a touch-and-go landing.

Three green lights winked on as the gear locked down.

The F-16 curved round in a steep descending turn on to finals. As we came round on to finals it became apparent that there was a strong crosswind from the right. We were crabbed slightly against the crosswind down final approach, then without fuss we were down, although the narrow-track gear meant that judicious use of aileron and rudder was needed to keep straight in the crosswind.

We had briefed for a touch-and-go and so the throttle went forward to the military power detent and the F-16 leaped off the ground again. The red light in the gear handle winked out as the doors closed. Fergione curved us round in a tight turn over the south base, setting us up for our final landing.

Again a tight turn on to finals. Then something unexpected. The MASTER CAUTION light on the coaming started to flash.

'That'll be the forward fuel,' said Fergione. 'That's normal at these fuel states.' I glanced down. Sure enough the FORWARD FUEL light on the right hand console was illuminated, showing that we were down to 250lb in the forward tank group.

In deference to the gusty conditions, Fergione flew the approach at eleven units AoA, rather faster than the thirteen AoA approach in the flight manual. He explained that the thirteen unit approach equated to a speed of 133 knots at this fuel weight but could result in a certain amount of wallowing on the approach in gusty conditions. This approach worked as advertised. We touched, and Fergione kept the nose up for aerodynamic braking as the speed dropped down to eighty knots.

The F-16 was an impressive fighter. Smaller by far than the huge F-15 Eagle, it could give a very good account of itself. It was a very enjoyable and productive flight, and one which showed to good effect the latest fighter in Air Force service.

27
The Ultimate War Machine

High over the desert, the MiG 21 was a silver delta-winged shape, framed in the softly green glowing symbols of my Head-Up Display (HUD). In the cockpit of the McDonnell Douglas F/A-18 Hornet I armed a Sparrow missile. The display changed modes as the radar locked on. A SHOOT command appeared and I pressed the trigger on the stick. The missile whooshed away, a smoke-trail arrowing out after the distant MiG. Five seconds later that MiG silently exploded in a ball of flame.

Turning back on course for my target, an industrial complex well into enemy territory, I made a single switch selection which brought up the attack displays. Through the HUD the target came into view, my weapons system already indicating the spot where the bombs would hit. I checked that the bombs were armed and ready to drop before rolling in for a steep dive attack from ten thousand feet. At three thousand feet the HUD commanded weapon release and I pulled out at less than one thousand feet, accelerating away over the desert in afterburner to Mach 0.9 to exit the target area at low level and high speed to evade the defences. Behind me with unerring accuracy the bombs erupted in the centre of the target.

Climbing up to altitude, I reselected the displays for the air-to-air mode. I turned, the hunter looking for its prey.

High overhead there was a flash of sunlight on wings as another MiG rolled in to the attack. Catching the flash of light in my peripheral vision I pulled the Hornet into a hard turn to the left. Overshooting, the MiG shot across my bows.

Momentarily losing sight of the MiG, I pulled harder, the Hornet protesting and buffeting while I craned to look over my shoulder to reacquire the MiG. Harder still, and my vision started dimming under the effect of the high g-forces as I hovered on the edge of a black-out. Using stick and rudder I rolled the Hornet quickly from side to side to find the deadly Mig. Still no sight of the enemy fighter and with a growing dread I realised that he must be in my blind spot at my six o'clock. The hunter was now the hunted.

This thought was punctuated by the unearthly sound of cannon fire as the MiG blasted the Hornet and everything went black.

There was an innocuous click and the lights came back on. 'Don't feel so bad about it,' said Captain Bob Knoy, standing by the side of the simulator cockpit, 'that's about average for a non-fighter pilot the first time. We start

149

off with an easy target for our pilots who have just come on to the Hornet. As their Air Combat Manoeuvring [ACM] training progresses, we introduce them to more difficult targets. Our computer is programmed with five levels of difficulty. The one that shot you down was a Level Five manoeuvring target, the most difficult. Level Five is Top Gun standard.'

I climbed shakily out of the cockpit. We were perched on a platform inside one of the forty-foot diameter domes of the Weapons Tactics Trainer at Marine Corps Air Station El Toro, in California. Although the computer had now frozen the action, it was still an extremely realistic scene projected on the inner face of the dome. The computer-derived MiG now flew formation with the Hornet against the blue sky, with the desert landscape, rimmed by a jagged mountain skyline, some two miles beneath us.

There was a lot to learn about the Hornet. The Hornet was a sophisticated dual-role supersonic fighter attack aircraft. In mastering the complex weapons systems of the F/A-18, the Navy and Marine pilots underwent comprehensive combat training in this simulator without the necessity of actual flight operations and the expenditure of fuel and the very expensive missiles. ACM could also be practised without risk to aircraft or pilot.

Giving the pilot actual experience of the mission or task in the simulator before he had to do it in the air proved a tremendous advantage. Marine pilots who had not flown the Hornet for fourteen days were required to fly the simulator before they flew the aircraft again.

I was impressed. The systems of the Hornet were complex, but very effective. In combat, the Hornet pilot could operate all the necessary systems from switches and buttons on the stick and throttles. This awesome capability required a manual dexterity which had been described as more appropriate to a clarinet player than to a fighter jock. There was no disputing that the training was intensive.

Talking to the Marine Hornet pilots, I asked them how they liked the aircraft. They just grinned. The nearest I got to an answer was from one crew-cutted Marine pilot who said firmly, 'No one has traded a Hornet in yet.'

But you could see it in their eyes. To a man, they all had Hornet fever.

This attitude was understandable. Pilots jealously defend their favourite aircraft. I was no different in that respect. At weekends for fun I was flying a Pitts Special. This pugnacious, cocky biplane had a snarling 260hp engine which would try to swing the aircraft off the runway at the slightest provocation. The Pitts had character. It sat on the ramp, barrel-chested and resplendent in its red, white and blue paint scheme, daring you to fly it. But once in the air it was a magical machine. The controls were feather-light, so sensitive that a thought was enough to send you twisting and turning through space. The Pitts had a special place in my affections.

150

I had flown a variety of aircraft, ranging from seaplanes to jets, from vintage biplanes to warbirds.

But there was one aircraft I dearly wanted to fly.

It was the hottest ship in the US inventory – the F/A-18 Hornet.

One day, the phone rang. It was the Pentagon. 'Would you like to fly a Hornet?'

Would a fish like to swim?

This was the first time a non-military British pilot had been given the opportunity to fly the Hornet.

In order to experience the Hornet at first hand, I was invited by the Department of the Navy to visit NAS Lemoore, near Fresno. Strike Fighter Squadron 125, the west coast training squadron for Hornets, was a unique organisation, operating under a dual command structure with personnel split between Navy and Marines. The duality was complete. The aircraft had NAVY stencilled on the right side of the fuselage, MARINES on the left side.

There was one snag. Before being permitted near this aircraft, I was put through a baptism of fire worthy of the Marquis de Sade. After a rigorous medical examination came water survival training. Try swimming a couple of lengths of an Olympic-sized pool wearing forty pounds of waterlogged flight gear. My instructor had forbidden me to inflate my life preserver. As my boots filled with water and my life flashed before my eyes, I began to wonder why I had volunteered.

Next came a trip in a high-altitude chamber. A rubber glove, tied at the wrist, hung on a string from the ceiling of the chamber. At sea level the glove was flaccid. Breathing through an oxygen mask I sat on a bench with other pilots on refresher training. As air was pumped out the atmosphere in the chamber became as thin as that found at the summit of Mount Everest. The air inside the glove had expanded and the glove was now bulging. Our instructor, evilly twirling his moustache, then instructed us to 'Take off your masks.' My subsequent observation that our instructor also had horns and a tail was no doubt a result of the hallucinations common to victims of hypoxia.

To dispel any doubts that this was a serious business, I was then given a ride on an ejection-seat rig which blasted me out of a dummy fuselage. Rubbing an aching neck, I consoled myself with the thought that those who happened to survive this course of refined torture were actually allowed to fly in the Hornet.

Kitted out in flight suit, life preserver and g-suit, I waddled out to the ramp at NAS Lemoore early on a hot summer morning to make my first acquaintance with the Hornet. My pilot was Captain Rich 'Ski' Karwowski, USMC. The Lemoore ramp was crowded with single- and two-seat Hornets and I was struck by the lack of ground equipment round each aircraft. Starting was accomplished by an APU built into each Hornet, thereby eliminating the

151

clutter of ground equipment necessary to launch previous generations of tactical jets. A pair of groundcrew was sufficient to launch each F/A-18.

The Hornet was a wicked-looking aircraft, with the leading edge extensions giving a sinister hooded look to the aircraft when seen from head on. This was certainly not the average run-of-the-mill piece of machinery.

While Captain Karwowski pre-flighted our F/A-18B, I climbed up the integral ladder, over the portside leading edge extension and into the rear cockpit. Our female crew chief assisted me in strapping into the Martin-Baker ejection seat. My four-point torso harness was connected, then the leg restraints, g-suit, oxygen and intercom connections. Conscious that I was sitting on a rocket-powered seat which would blast me out of the aircraft in case of serious trouble, I made sure that my kneepad was well clear of the actuating handle at the front of the seat. For this two-ship training mission our callsign was RAIDER 55, while RAIDER 58 was an F/A-18 single-seater flown by Captain Ron 'Buzz' Berlie, Canadian Armed Forces, on an exchange posting with the US Navy.

I took stock of the spacious rear cockpit. The rear cockpit of the Hornet was equipped with three Multi-Function Displays (MFDs). The HUD display seen by the front-seat pilot was repeated on my left MFD, with a navigational display on my centre MFD and a pre-start checklist on the right hand display.

Once Captain Karwowski was aboard, the ladder was folded away into the underside of the LEX and the left engine was started. The digital engine instruments wound up and a pre-flight controls menu appeared on the right hand MFD. With the second engine running, the aircraft went through an automatic test sequence, with much thumping and shaking from the control surfaces. Spreading our hands outside the canopy rails, away from all switches, we waited while our crew chief checked underneath the aircraft, then we taxied out, following RAIDER 58 to the head of the 13,500-foot runway.

Once the canopy was closed we pulled close to RAIDER 58 on his right hand side. Buzz would be leading us for a military power take-off. As our engines spooled up to 100 per cent, at a nod of the helmet from the other cockpit the brakes were released and the two Hornets accelerated down the runway. At 145 knots we rotated and climbed in formation, turning eastwards towards the spine of the Sierra Nevada. We widened out into battle formation and Rich gave me control of the Hornet.

Let me digress a bit here. In battle formation, the idea is to keep far enough apart to cover the other pilot's six o'clock to make sure no bandits can bounce him. So we were some distance apart as I settled down and got used to the highly sensitive hydraulically powered flight controls of the Hornet. It was almost as sensitive as the Pitts, but the last serious formation flying I had done was when I was piloting the camera ship for a photographic sortie between two light aircraft. On that occasion my aircraft weighed 1,500lb and I had 150 horsepower to play with.

Our Hornet, RAIDER 55, was loaded to the gills with internal fuel and an external tank. It weighed in at around 34,000lb. The twin throttles down on the left console controlled a pair of General Electric F404 turbofans whose maximum thrust translated to something over fifty thousand horse-power in afterburner when the aircraft was travelling at supersonic speed. So this ship was not quite the same as the average light aircraft. After a few exploratory curves and switchbacks I managed to keep us in the same piece of sky as RAIDER 58.

We neared the spectacular backdrop of the Sierra Nevada, still snow-covered on this summer day in spite of the 100F degree heat back at Lemoore. It was an awesome view on this cloudless day and the visibility from the rear seat of the Hornet was outstanding under the bubble canopy. I handed control back to Rich and looked down to check my oxygen.

I looked up when a shadow fell across my cockpit.

There's formation flying, and there's *formation flying*. This was *formation flying*.

This was the way the Blue Angels performed. This was regular military close formation flying. At this point the other Hornet was seemingly welded just off our left side, with the wingtip and its Sidewinder missile rail a couple of feet away from our cockpit, so close that I could count the rivets in the missile rail which was almost near enough to touch.

The two Hornets zipped around the snow-covered summit of Mount Whitney while in the background a female voice warned, 'Altitude, altitude' as the ground rose beneath us. This audio warning was one piece of the Star Wars gadgetry in the Hornet. Driven by the radar altimeter, like sonar in a boat, this device warned of rising ground beneath us.

RAIDER 58 broke away and floated off into the distance to complete his own airwork, while we headed for Panamint Valley, a huge dry lakebed to the east of the Sierra Nevada, rimmed by saw-toothed mountains.

My turn again and cleared to 30,000 feet I climbed initially at constant airspeed, showing a 6,000ft/min rate of climb on the HUD, then switched to a Mach number profile.

At 28,500 feet I levelled out to assess the low speed handling. Rich brought up the controls display on the right hand MFD. I retarded both throttles. As I slowed down, the flaps were in auto mode and the display showed the leading edge flaps programming down while the trailing edge flaps came up. Unlocking my shoulder harness, and twisting round, I could see the leading edge flaps now fully down on the wing, some way behind me.

As I monitored the HUD repeater indications, I was steadily bringing the

153

power up as the drag increased. Angle of attack was increasing. As speed dropped through 150 knots we entered buffeting which got progressively heavier until the Sidewinder rails at the wingtips were visibly shaking. I continued slowing the Hornet to 120 knots. This gave a thirty degree nose up pitch angle. Both throttles were now up to military power and yet we were gradually descending because the induced drag was so high.

At this point Rich said, 'See what lateral control is like . . . without using rudder.'

Did I hear correctly? In over twenty years of flying I've learned and in turn taught that in slow flight you *always* use the rudder; you never use aileron near the stall, lest you provoke a stall on one wing and roll yourself inverted.

'Without using rudder?'

'Sure.'

I gingerly moved the stick to the left. The left wing went smoothly down to forty-five degrees, then stopped as I centralised the stick. We were still flying, although the ride was uncomfortable, like riding an unsprung cart over a washboard road. I moved the stick to the right. Obediently the Hornet reversed its bank and we turned to the right.

Any other aircraft would have been spinning wildly by now. 'Look at the display,' Rich said. I looked at the controls display and remembered. The Hornet had a fly-by-wire digital flight control system. Built in to the computer was a spin protection circuit. At low speeds any aileron input was automatically washed out. As the display showed, the horizontal stabilators, leading edge flaps and vertical rudders were all moving to roll the aircraft, with the ailerons remaining undeflected. Turning round I watched everything move as I twitched the stick. It was a humbling experience to realise that the computers could fly better than any human pilot at this flight condition.

We descended to 19,000 feet to demonstrate some Air Combat Manoeuvring (ACM). First came a horizontal scissors, to force an opponent to overshoot. Starting from 150 knots in afterburner, Rich pulled the nose up to sixty degrees. We came out of burner and the stick went fully forward as the throttles slammed back to flight idle. A negative alpha warning tone sounded in my headset. My feet tried to float off the pedals as we arced over the top at no more than ninety knots.

In contrast to earlier aircraft the Hornet had no restrictions on throttle movement. The rugged F404s responded well to this harsh treatment. By now our sudden stop would have caused our imaginary opponent to overshoot in front of us.

At 140 knots we commenced a split S, lighting afterburners and rolling inverted, pulling full aft stick to pull back into level flight at the same speed but a mere couple of thousand feet lower on a reciprocal heading. Not many opponents could follow that.

Next came a high-g evasive manoeuvre. With an imaginary bogie at our seven o'clock, both afterburners were lit and we snapped into a steep left turn, rapidly pulling to 6.6g. This started an out-of-plane manoeuvre to get us away from the bandit's nose. The pitch rate was impressive. At this point I weighed over half a ton and it felt as if I'd been jumped on by an elephant.

Immediate application of bottom rudder started our nose corkscrewing down towards the lakebed floor, then a continued pull brought our nose up above the horizon in pursuit of our imaginary target. This ability of the Hornet to swap ends rapidly was disconcerting to any adversary and had caused embarrassment on a number of occasions when other aircraft had attempted ACM against Hornets for the first time.

In the space of about five minutes we covered the complete gamut of Air Combat Manoeuvres between ninety knots and 400 knots.

In this apparently limitless blue bowl above the desert, there was a lot of traffic. Now a pair of targets appeared on the scope and we locked onto them with the radar. As we got closer, we initially saw a pair of smoke trails, then the pair of grey F-4s as they slid across the jagged mountain backdrop below. We would have splashed them both.

So far I had seen the F/A-18 Hornet in its F (Fighter) role. How about the A (Attack)?

We dropped down towards the edge of Panamint Valley, skirting the outer rim of the mountains rimming the valley. Again that 'Altitude' warning sounded in our ears. Rich switched the radar to the ground mapping mode and the radar began to paint the rising ground in front of us. A notch in the lunar landscape in front of us was Rainbow Canyon, a sinuous sheer-sided valley which ran down to the lakebed. We entered the canyon, descending below the rim for maximum cover. At 400 knots and pulling 3g round each convolution of the riverbed we whistled down the canyon. The ride inside the Hornet was impressively quiet and smooth. In mere seconds we descended the length of the canyon, emerging 1,000 feet above the lakebed into Panamint Valley itself, maintaining altitude by radar altimeter. We were now loitering at 200 knots and looking for trouble, multi-mode radar searching for targets on the ground. Throttles went forward to the military power detent and we accelerated effortlessly to 300 knots before going into afterburner. We continued to accelerate, with a growing whine from the canopy above 500 knots. My digital readout on the display flickered up to 600 knots, the cockpit still uncannily quiet as the desert blurred past outside at over a thousand feet a second.

To prevent us going supersonic and decimating the jackrabbit population with our shock wave, Rich pulled the nose up and, sitting on the twin arrows of flame crackling from our jetpipes, we soared up and over into a giant loop, coming back to military power and topping out inverted at 24,000 feet.

We were still fat with fuel, with ten minutes before we were due to rendezvous with RAIDER 58 for the homeward flight. Rich rolled us out from inverted, raised his gloved hands from the stick and throttles and said, 'OK, it's your airplane.'

What do you do when you are given control of eighteen million dollars worth of fighting machine? First of all you gingerly take hold of the button-encrusted stick with your right hand. Secondly, your left hand wraps around those hefty throttles. Thirdly, I must admit, under your oxygen mask, you start grinning. Walter Mitty never had it so good.

So here I was, sitting under a bubble canopy, under a cloudless deep blue sky, while on the instrument panel three green displays gave a good imitation of a Star Wars control room whilst monitoring our progress. The left hand display was a repeater for the pilot's head-up display, with airspeed, altitude and g, together with a few other flight parameters. Our radar was busy painting airborne targets on the right-hand scope. On the central MFD a navigation display pinpointed our position with uncanny accuracy over Panamint Valley. I confirmed this by looking out to see the Sierra Nevada stretching majestically to the horizon off our left wing as we headed north. With the shoulder harness unlocked I could turn round and see the twin verticals some way behind me.

I hesitated, then asked, 'Anything I shouldn't do?'

Older jets were hedged around with airspeed and g-force limitations. Rich shrugged, then shook his head, 'Just fly it like a Pitts.'

The statement was not so casual as it appeared. The Hornet's computer-driven flight controls included a sophisticated g-limiting system which would back off on the controls if an over-zealous pilot tried to pull round a corner too hard. This could otherwise bend the airplane. Even so, Hornet pilots were very aware of blacking themselves out as the aircraft could then take more gs than the pilots.

I started with a few basic aerobatic manoeuvres. An Immelmann first, initiated from 350 knots. I pushed both throttles forward through the detent at military power and through into full afterburner. There was a dull rumble from somewhere behind me and a strong shove in my back as the afterburners lit. I brought the stick back, intending to keep the pull-up in the loop to 4g, but the Hornet was so responsive that I overdid it, with the g-meter reading an accusing 5.4g on the display. The g-suit inflated hard, squeezing my thighs and abdomen. Floating over the top of the loop, as the horizon slid down under the nose I pushed forward until we were in level flight, then moved the stick sideways and rolled out to complete the Immelmann turn. The controls were light and precise.

Rich said, 'Want to try a split S?'

For the split S I slowed to 140 knots, heading south, then selected full afterburner and rolled inverted, pulling the stick full aft to get the nose pitching down at this low speed. My display told me that we were now snow-ploughing through the air, forcing the wing through the air at thirty-five degrees to the relative airflow even though the nose was pointing straight down towards the salt flats of Panamint Valley. As we fell like a rock towards the desert the engines' thrust balanced the tremendous drag. An audio warning beeped in my ears . . . don't pull any harder. The whole aircraft was buffeting in protest, and the speed remained uncannily stabilised at 140 knots.

Unbelievably, to one used to previous generation jets which used miles of airspace to carry out a manoeuvre, as we hammered round into level flight, heading north again, our Hornet was only 2,000 feet lower than when we started. It was an awesome display of the capability of the aircraft. In a classic dogfight even the Red Baron would have had trouble following that manoeuvre. Coming out of afterburner, we continued accelerating to 400 knots with only the green digits on the HUD confirming the speed change.

I pushed the stick a couple of inches over to the left and playfully rolled the Sierras around us. Once we were level again I tried a full deflection roll, banging the stick over until it hit my knee. The Hornet zipped round with alacrity at over 200 degrees/second. Control was precise and instantaneous. As I centred the stick we flipped back into level flight. In this aircraft the roll rate was limited by the neck-snapping acceleration on the unfortunate crew.

I tried wingovers and reversals between 300 and 150 knots. These were just plain fun as we wheeled and soared above the mountains. It was only when the g-suit inflated that I realised I was pulling nearly 4g during this series of manoeuvres. A single-handed pull at 300 knots gave an effortless 6g. Low-speed handling was remarkable. Behaviour was viceless and the handling was more appropriate to a light aircraft like the Pitts than a heavy tactical jet.

All too soon it was time to go back to work.

We locked up the radar on a head-on target at twenty-eight miles. A minute or so later I picked up the target visually as it flashed down our right side some two thousand feet below. It was a Hornet. Grey-painted and with smokeless engines the Hornet was much more difficult to acquire visually than the F-4s.

Then our radar picked up RAIDER 58. I was flying at 20,000 feet over the Sierras when RAIDER 58 appeared and slid into close formation on our right side. Engaging the ALTITUDE HOLD mode of the autopilot lowered my workload as I tried the various radar modes. The radar controls on the throttle made it simple to vary the search elevation of the radar and to move the cursor on the screen. Switching from air-to-air to air-to-ground, the ground mapping capability of the APG-65 radar built up a picture of Fresno.

157

Individual roads could be seen. The picture could be frozen and zoomed at will. Following the computer-generated symbol of the IN system, we led RAIDER 58 back to Lemoore and broke for individual landings.

Following normal Navy practice, all landings at Lemoore were done as simulated carrier landings. Rich Karwowski followed the meatball of the mirror landing sight down to a purposely firm touchdown on the carrier deck painted on the runway, before spooling up the engines to get us airborne again. On the downwind leg Rich went to full afterburner to demonstrate graphically the acceleration at light weight. My helmet slammed back against the headrest as we accelerated like a dragster up to three hundred and fifty knots. Before we rocketed out of state he cut afterburner and brought the Hornet round on final approach. Rock steady on approach we touched down for a short landing with anti-skid braking cycling, speed brake raised and stabilisers fully deflected to slow our speed.

The Hornet was typical of the latest generation of all-weather attack aircraft, but additionally was a hell of a fighter, flying as often as not from the pitching deck of an aircraft carrier. Flying qualities were exceptional, the capability of the weapons system was awesome. The ultimate war machine.

28
Biplane Reprise

Chino, in southern California, is another of those magic airports which exist, like Aladdin's cave, for the delight of the soul. Among the hangars on any weekend one can find Mustangs, a Swedish Draken, Sabres and all kinds of strange aircraft. However, the majority of pilots fly aircraft more suited to average pockets.

A clearing mist shrouded the perimeter of the field as a Stearman biplane was pulled out of the hangar. A silver N2S-5, this 220hp version was in complete contrast to the sophisticated jets I had been flying.

Pre-flighting this biplane was necessarily a leisurely affair. The fabric-covered wings and empennage looked OK. The engine was the most complex item. One by one I checked the exposed plug leads on the radial engine. Then the oil. Hangar lore said if the Lycoming was dripping oil, it was OK . . . the time to worry was when the ground underneath the engine was dry. As I looked at the state of the oil-spattered concrete we seemed to have a sufficiency of oil. Nevertheless I climbed up on the port main wheel, unscrewed the oil filler cap and pulled out the dipstick. With nearly four gallons indicated, the oil level was OK. I jumped back down off the wheel.

As this was the first flight of the day the wooden propeller was turned laboriously through eighteen blades to clear the oil from the lower cylinders. Then I gave five strokes of the pump on the left hand cowling to prime the engine.

I swung back up onto the wing walkway, and carefully climbed on board, being careful of the fabric on wings and fuselage side when entering the leather-rimmed rear cockpit. Once my feet were on the floorboards, I wriggled down into the seat and carefully went through the ritual of donning the parachute and seat harness. It was a simple but roomy cockpit, designed to accept the bulkiest trainee pilot wearing heavy flight gear.

My hands and eyes worked together as I reacquainted myself with this simpler and older form of levitation. I checked from left to right around the cockpit. The trim lever down on the left of my seat was set for take-off, and on the power quadrant the throttle was closed and the mixture lever set to RICH. Further forward, the gust lock lever was disengaged and the fuel was on.

Then on to the panel. Magnetos were off, altimeter and engine instruments were OK, with the old E2B compass floating serenely behind its glass

159

window. The radio on the right hand wall was the only concession to the modern day world of aviation. During this time I was becoming aware of the unique smell of leather, dope and fabric unique to old aircraft. It was a different age of flying.

One last look round and I was ready to go. Flipping the master switch on, I cracked the throttle open and pulled the stick back. With brakes set, I was clear to start. I turned the starter key and a rising wail assaulted my ears as the inertia starter began to wind up. When I heard the pitch flattening out, the flywheel had reached maximum speed and I pulled the starting T-handle on the right side of the panel.

The big wooden prop kicked over. There was a coughing roar from the engine and a blast of blue-grey smoke out of the big exhaust collector stack on the right side of the engine.

As I checked that oil temperature and pressure were rising, the big radial engine settled down into a steady grumbling roar. Time to check with the tower and taxi out. Taxiing out in this taildragger required lots of weaving and stabbing at the brakes to maintain some semblance of visibility. I slowly made my way out to the main taxi-way, slotting in between a P-51 Mustang and an SBD Dauntless from the Planes of Fame museum further up the field.

There was a momentary feeling of déjà vu. It was an eerie sensation, as I realised that momentarily there were only 1940s era military aircraft in sight. Perhaps it was a time warp, the first step into the twilight zone . . .

Dragging myself back to the task at hand, I ruddered the Stearman into the run-up area, ran up the engine against the brakes and checked the magnetos and the carb heat. As usual I muttered imprecations against the designer who hid the carb heat lever in the recesses of the fuselage; it required a good stretch to reach the carb heat lever, easier from the front cockpit than the rear.

By the time I had finished, the Mustang was howling past on his take-off. I switched to tower frequency and got clearance to take off, did a final check of the controls, released the brakes and rumbled onto the runway.

Lining up as best I could because of the atrocious visibility from the back seat, and keeping my feet off the brakes, I opened the throttle. The idling prop vanished in a blur and a wave of sound erupted from the exhaust.

The Stearman needed right rudder to keep straight. I eased the stick forward. Once the tail came up, visibility improved dramatically. There was a tremendous racket from the open exhaust, the struts and the flying wires adding to the cacophony of sound as the Stearman decided to fly and lifted off the runway.

With the speed up to 70 mph in the climb, I throttled back and slowly the Stearman climbed above the haze layer. It was crystal clear above, with the San Gabriel mountains forming a backdrop to the north as I lazily circled.

It was summer and the air was warm even with the 80 mph wind rushing past. It was great fun. Navigating by following roads and railroad tracks, I flew down to Lake Mathews, turning over the mirror-like lake.

After a few minutes sightseeing it was time to head back to the field.

Nearing Chino a black speck appeared in front of the biplane, one of the ubiquitous hawks that abound in this area. He refused to budge at the approach of this noisy interloper into his domain, just continued circling in a thermal. Flight feathers outspread, the hawk ignored me, so I jinked right and went round him. I frowned as a voice intruded on my small world. It was the tower, warning me that the Mustang was coming back into the pattern. I searched to my right. There he was, speeding along, a silhouette in plan view already breaking into a right hand pattern. The Stearman continued to rumble downwind.

The Mustang, gear down, was slotting in on final approach to runway 21, which intersected the runway which I would be using. I came round on to final approach with the ASI quivering on seventy . . . don't crowd the Mustang . . . throttled back, and started S-turning, aiming to let the Mustang get in well in front. I peered past the clattering engine and the exposed cylinders to see the Mustang crossing a mile ahead of me. Now that the runway was clear, I could bring the throttle back and start descending. With the drag of those wires and struts, the Stearman came down like a brick once the throttle came back.

Near the ground, flying the Stearman always started to get interesting. During the flare, the runway vanished behind the engine and peripheral vision came into play. Judging the instant to flare consistently was easier said than done. The Stearman was a humbling machine and even very experienced pilots occasionally had trouble landing the beast.

It went quiet as the biplane floated above the runway. I brought the stick right back into my lap and the Stearman quit flying, with a squeak of tyres. Working hard on the rudder pedals to keep the biplane heading straight, I kept the stick back to force the tail down and keep some directional control. I had to remember not to touch the brakes, which would flip the Stearman on its nose in the twinkling of an eye. When the speed had dropped to walking pace, I gently ruddered off the runway and taxied back to the hangar.

Flying the Stearman was an unabashed return to the earlier age of flying. This open-cockpit aviating was a delight and completely different from the rigours of jet flying.

29

Practice Makes Perfect

As the orange ball of the sun heaved itself over the mountains to the east of the Imperial Valley in southern California, the first rays of the sun sparkled from canopies and polished skin. On the flight line six blue and gold Hornets were lined up precisely in a row. I had arrived here early at NAS El Centro, the winter training quarters for the Blue Angels, but the day had started hours previously for the team, with the crew chiefs starting with a 4.30 am inspection of their jets. By six o'clock Commander Gil Rud was already briefing the six-man team in their unpretentious wooden building.

Dawn had arrived this crisp March morning with a cloudless sky and unlimited visibility. All was going according to plan. The good winter weather and clear airspace was the raison d'être for the Blue Angels moving here from their base at Pensacola each year for winter training.

As briefing finished, three Navy crewmen stationed themselves at parade-ground readiness with each plane, two at the wingtips and a crew-chief at the nose. In front of Hornet #1, the leader's plane, the pilots lined up shoulder-to-shoulder in their blue flight suits. Lock-stepped together they marched out to their aircraft.

On reaching his own plane each pilot saluted his crew chief, turned out of line, climbed the ladder and swung into the cockpit. With the clock ticking, and all pilots aboard, in a burst of rising sound the engines started and in an intricately choreographed and synchronised ballet, the crew chiefs sema-phored the control surface movements of each ship. It was impressive. Every Blue Angel practice was treated as if a crowd of thousands were watching. This day the audience was smaller, consisting of the rest of the detachment, but their critical gaze promised no respite for any minor shortcomings.

Then the chocks were pulled away and with a burst of engine power Commander Rud's Hornet, identified by the stylised #1 on the verticals, pulled away, turning right onto the taxi-way. Immediately #2 started rolling and the remaining pair of the diamond four, then the two solo aircraft, fol-lowed in pairs to the head of the runway.

By 0800 hours the diamond four were airborne, sending waves of sound crackling across the field and the surrounding agricultural countryside. A moment later the two solo aircraft lifted off the runway. This was a prac-tice session for the whole team; pilots, groundcrew and the team narrator. While the narrator went into his patter, the diamond formation thundered

162

in from our left, changed formation into trail during a roll, then exited to our right.

For the next forty minutes they practised their display over the field, alternating their passes between the diamond of four, then the solos. Maybe twenty individual manoeuvres. Then they went through it again. The pressure was on with a vengeance as it was only a matter of days before the display season started. The performance looked good to me. But here in the blue skies over El Centro the team were honing their performance to perfection, practising over and over again.

But I was not at El Centro just to watch the Blue Angels fly. On this occasion I had been invited to fly in one of the Hornets. It was a rare privilege. This was the first time a British writer had flown with the Blue Angels.

Before the practice had finished I was kitted out with a blue flight suit, then briefed on ejection seat operation. The building shook as the final bomb-burst sent one Hornet blasting straight overhead.

The jets landed individually. Back on the ramp their arrival was treated as a display by all concerned. Once again the ground crew actions were synchronised with no visible sign of communication. In a synchronised sequence the pilots doffed their helmets, donned their caps and climbed down the ladders to the ramp as one man.

I was waiting in the maintenance office, crammed into the tiny room with the six crew chiefs, when the pilots entered. There was tension in the air. If all went well, I would fly in the spare aircraft – #7 – before the next full team performance scheduled for 1100 hours. A major snag discovered at this stage would require #7 to be substituted and my ride would be postponed.

To my relief, there were no major snags, although #4 – Donnie Cochran – complained of a failing radio to his female crew chief. This provoked a flurry of activity, with radio boxes scheduled to be rapidly replaced.

Meanwhile team leader Gil Rud was discussing with #2 the effect of a low level wind shear during the display just completed. Apparently on one of the tricky cross-over manoeuvres the wind difference between 200 feet and 600 feet altitude had been enough to affect the split-second timing, although not enough for the result to be apparent to an outsider.

I met the pilots in the four-ship diamond. Commander Gil Rud joined the Blue Angels in November 1985 and took the team through the transition from the A-4 to the vastly more sophisticated Hornet. His wingman in Hornet #2 was Captain Kevin Lauver, a Marine Pilot and a former Harrier driver, in his first year with the team. Left wing was flown by Lieutenant Commander Mark Ziegler, who previously flew Hornets with the East Coast Hornet training squadron VFA-106. Slot man, in the #4 ship, was Donnie Cochran, a former F-14 pilot and veteran Blue Angel, who flew left wing in the last A-4 season before transitioning to the Hornet in 1987.

For this season Lieutenant Wayne Molnar was lead solo. Lieutenant Cliff Skelton was opposing solo. The team's narrator, and my pilot in #7 for this sortie, would be Lt Doug McClain.

Assignment to the Blue Angels was extremely competitive, although selection did not require previous Hornet experience. Pilots were normally assigned to the Blue Angels for two years, but when the team transitioned to the Hornet, after thirteen years with the A-4, some pilots stayed on to ease the transition. These pilots were now entering their third season.

Since joining the team in October and November, the new pilots had qualified on the Hornet and at this point in time now had about 200 hours each in the aircraft. Their training started simply enough, using two airplanes at high altitude. Progressively, altitudes were decreased and more aircraft brought into the formation.

It was now March and two weeks before the first display of the season. By now about 150 flights had been completed. The display programme was daunting, with a total of seventy-five displays scheduled between April and October. It was a gruelling existence, with the team on the road for 300 days during the year.

The Blue Angels proudly boasted that they had never had to cancel a display through a mechanical failure. On the road they were largely self-sufficient and travelled with 'Fat Albert', a C-130 which carried the groundcrew and support equipment.

Six Hornets normally were assigned to the team, with one aircraft kept as a spare and plugged into a ground power unit, Inertial Navigation Unit aligned and ready to go.

A runway alert van carried a back-up crew of specialist technicians, in the event of anything going wrong between the ramp and the runway. Nothing was left to chance. On the road, many individuals had multiple jobs. It was a professional and motivated atmosphere, one which combined professionalism with showmanship to form the high-visibility point of the Navy's recruiting effort.

I met Doug McClain, a former A-6 pilot who flew the two-seat F/A-18B #7 in addition to his task of team narrator. We walked out to our Hornet for an 0930 start up. #7 stood at the end of the flightline. This Hornet, painted in glossy dark blue and gold, looked considerably slicker than the regular matt-grey attack Hornet which I had flown at NAS Lemoore.

Despite the fancy paintwork, the Blue Angel aircraft retained their avionics and radar. The only major modification was that a smoke-generating system was now mounted in the nose, replacing the standard 20mm cannon and ammunition tanks.

Climbing the ladder pivoted out of the portside LEX I lowered myself into the rear cockpit, strapping into the Martin-Baker seat. The first thing I noticed was that the harness was modified to give greater restraint during violent manoeuvres. Donning the gold helmet, trademark of the Blue Angels, I tightened the harness straps while Doug McClain climbed straight into the front seat, strapped in and started the APU.

This was another departure from the norm. Blue Angel pilots did not pre-flight their aircraft in the display environment. The crew chief for each air-craft bore the total responsibility for his machine. This trust was reflected by McClain's actions.

There was another feature peculiar to Blue Angels operations. Despite the high performance of the Hornet, the Blue Angels did not wear g-suits. Consequently the pilots kept in superb physical condition to counter the effects of the repeated high-g manoeuvres. They lifted weights, some of them ran, all were superb athletes. Flying twice every morning during winter training, the pilots kept their afternoons free for physical conditioning. This should have been a warning for this largely desk-bound writer, who only flew aerobatics at weekends . . .

The Star Wars cockpit of the Hornet came to life as the APU brought the electrics on line. At exactly 0930 a calm female voice started incongruously to recite the various audio warnings in my earphones: 'Left engine fire . . . APU fire . . .'

The digital fuel counter down by my left knee confirmed that we had 9,800lb of JP-5 on board. We mutually checked in on the intercom. No oxygen masks would be needed during our low-level mission, so we would use the lighter boom microphones.

As the right engine lit and whined up to sixty-three per cent the three Multi-Function Displays in my cockpit came alive. I noticed that one display showed that we had a 7g limit on the aircraft at our fuel weight. Then the Built-In Test sequence for the flight controls started. This progress was shown on both left and right screens in concert with much thumping from behind me as the computer drove the various control surfaces automatically through their full ranges in a predetermined sequence. The flight controls checked out OK.

My displays changed as McClain selected a pre-take-off checklist on the left hand display. Navigational information was on the centre display. Even our weight of some 34,300lb was displayed.

'Hands in?' asked McClain, and I tucked my elbows in as the big bubble canopy sighed down, then slid forward and locked. A burst of power got us moving with nosewheel steering helping us to negotiate the sharp turns on the taxi-way.

At the head of the runway we lined up. McClain received permission from the tower for a maximum performance take-off. Warning bells started to go off in my head. I watched the throttles go forward for a power check. As the digital gauges spun up to eighty-five per cent the nose dipped under the thrust of the two F404 engines. My displays changed again as McClain switched displays so that his HUD information was repeated on my left hand screen.

I could hear my own breathing. One last look around the cockpit. Everything was in order and McClain released the brakes and pushed the throttles forward into the afterburner range. Our gauges showed that both nozzles opened and then both burners lit.

'Blowers look OK,' said McClain laconically.

There was a rumble behind me and an inexorable acceleration pushed me back into my seat. My eyes were fixed on the rapidly changing and green-glowing numbers of the HUD as thirty-two thousand pounds of thrust made the Hornet accelerate down the runway like a drag racer. We were barely a thousand feet down the runway when 130 knots appeared on the HUD and a slight backward movement on the stick got us airborne. As the gear retracted and the gear doors snapped shut, McClain held the Hornet down and the speed really started to wind up. As the end of the runway flashed beneath we were accelerating through three hundred and fifty knots.

'Here we go,' said McClain and pulled back on the stick. Braced in anticipation against the g-force, I nevertheless felt my cheeks sag, my helmet dramatically get heavier and my peripheral vision started to fade. As the greyness progressively reduced my vision I strained against the g-force, con-centrating on the HUD to see 5g as we continued pulling to the vertical.

As the Hornet rocketed upwards, normal vision returned as the g-force reduced. 'Look over your shoulder,' said McClain. I twisted round and looked back past the twin tails to see the plan view of NAS El Centro reced-ing at a dizzying rate. Still climbing vertically, McClain rolled the Hornet ninety degrees to the right and pulled through to inverted. Passing through five thousand feet we came out of burner, rolled upright and turned left to exit the pattern, heading for the desert range near Superstition Mountain where the practice aerobatic area was located.

Only then did I remember to breathe again.

Visibility was excellent from the rear seat. We were flying in a cloudless blue sky with mountains rimming the horizon. As the irrigated agricultural areas and the runways of El Centro receded behind the tail of the Hornet, I looked around.

The blue expanse of the Salton Sea lay off to the north, while below was a lunar landscape of sandy desert and raw rock. Moments later we were over-head our practice display areas. There was little to set it apart from the miles of featureless and rugged desert. An ersatz runway had been scraped out across the dirt while an orange-painted trailer acted as show centre.

Just to warm up, Doug McClain did a couple of aileron rolls, then invited me to try the same manoeuvre. No sweat, I'd done this before in the Hornet. As my hand moved the stick a couple of inches to the right the horizon whirled. The Hornet slammed into the roll much faster than I had anticipated. Too late I remembered that this Hornet carried no fuel-laden centre-line external tank to slow the roll rate. By the time I centralised the stick we had rotated through 360 degrees and were more or less upright again.

I licked my lips, gently held the stick between thumb and forefinger and tried a gentler approach. Aileron rolls to left and right to start with. Then progressing to four-point and eight-point rolls, rapidly becoming attuned to the sensitivity of the hydraulic flight control system. By now we were nearing the edge of our reserved airspace and I pulled into a 4g turn to reverse our course. Lack of a g-suit was bearable, now that I was flying the Hornet, although straining against the prolonged application of g-forces as we completed the course reversal was proving more difficult than I had anticipated.

'I'll show you how we normally fly a display,' said McClain. 'We have a 15lb downspring that we hook into the pitch control system. This takes out any slop and gives more margin for trimming in inverted flight.'

As he connected this spring into the system, the stick tried to move forward and bury itself in the panel. So I had to pull back against that 15lb force just to stay in level flight. It was not too bad at first as I tried more rolls and wing-overs. But over the next few minutes, as I constantly manoeuvred between 3 and 4g just to keep within our proscribed airspace, the physical effort just to keep the Hornet turning was noticeably increased. McClain said drily, 'Blue Angel pilots develop strong right arms.'

As advertised, the inverted capability of the Hornet was good. When I rolled the Hornet upside down, if I relaxed the back pressure the aircraft even tended to climb. All Blue Angel Hornets had been modified to have forty-five seconds of inverted capability. If fuel pressure dropped, a warning light would give a five-second warning of impending flameout. (This was small comfort. One solo pilot the previous year had been forced to eject when he cut the margin too close and both engines quit on him during practice over this exact spot.)

Not wishing to see if the light worked, I tried a couple of shorter inverted runs, just long enough to show me that the Hornet handled well while inverted.

My modified harness included a lap belt, thigh restraints, shoulder straps and a chest strap. When all was snugged down correctly, even prolonged inverted flight was not uncomfortable.

This was fun.

Eventually I rolled back upright, then immediately had to bank into another steep turn as we approached the limits of our airspace, marked by another range of mountains. By this time it was becoming a chore to be constantly pulling back against the 15lb of nose-down trim in addition to the normal stick force of maybe twenty pounds required during each 4g course reversal. Despite positioning the air vents to blow cold air on me, perspiration was running down into my eyes and my right arm was on fire. Finally McClain took pity on me, unhitched the spring and we reverted back to the standard pitch control system for some vertical manoeuvres.

I started with a half Cuban eight, a half loop followed by a descending roll. Maintaining line on the way up was complicated in the Hornet because the wings were way behind the cockpit, so normal cues were absent. On the other hand, with no propeller scything the air out front there was no torque to pull the nose off line. Momentarily weightless I floated over the top, pointed the nose downhill and rolled out as the desert started to expand towards us.

Next came a loop. Trying to aim for the recommended ten AoA on the HUD and pulling up into the sun, I found the pitch control was sensitive and overshot to 5g during the pull-up. But the Hornet was forgiving and again we floated over the top, whistling down the far side of the loop without fuss.

Once we were straight and level, McClain said, 'I'll show you a minimum radius loop. It's an eye-watering experience in this aircraft.'

He accelerated to four hundred and fifty knots as we approached show centre. Anticipating what was coming I braced for the onset of the g-force. As the trailer slid below the nose, the stick came right back in my lap. Concentrating on the g-meter I read 7.3 before the lights went out. I could still hear my breathing and feel the aircraft buffeting, but it was only as g reduced fractionally as we were inverted at the top of the loop that my vision suddenly returned, with the instrument panel appearing in monochrome for an instant, then flashing back into full colour, just as McClain asked solicitously, 'Still with me?' I grunted out an affirmative, but then my vision went completely at 7g again in the pull-out, not returning completely until we pulled out into level flight. Eye-watering, you bet. The pitch capability of the Hornet was awesome, with the diameter of the loop around 3,500 feet.

McClain then handed the Hornet back to me and we accelerated back to 450 knots to set up for a maximum rate climb. 'We might go supersonic on this one,' said McClain conversationally. The area was clear and I rolled over the vertical and headed down for show centre. McClain took over as we descended and we really started motoring as the throttles went all the way forward. The GE F404s were impressive, showing no signs of distress during all of our drastic manoeuvres.

We arrived at show centre, pulling up to the vertical in a 5g pull-up in buffet and slight wing rock. As the nose reached the zenith, momentarily we both saw the rate of climb peak at 51,200 ft/min. The desert dropped rapidly away below us. Still in this exhilarating vertical climb, McClain rolled the aircraft through 360 degrees, then pulled to inverted at 15,000 feet to complete our aerobatic session. As we rolled upright I took over again, glad of the respite to let my protesting stomach settle down as we leisurely cruised over the southern end of the Salton Sea.

The high technology used in these modern fighters was a mixed blessing. One problem was that the Hornet, with its quiet cockpit and auto-trim of the computerised flight control system, lacked the speed cues taken for granted by previous generations of pilots. So the pilot had to rely on his instruments, particularly the HUD. I started letting down using the HUD, levelled at 7,500 feet, then reversed course towards El Centro while McClain demonstrated the radar by picking up targets of aircraft in the pattern. We stepped down to 3,500 feet and Lieutenant McClain took us back into the pattern for a 7.3g break from over 500 knots. That was another eye-watering experience.

As soon as we had climbed out, Hornet #7 was refuelled. An hour later, with the radios on #4 still sick, #7 became the slot aircraft for the second team display of the day. The diamond this time did a spectacular formation 'burner loop' on take-off before vanishing over the desert to the practice area.

With the high thrust-to-weight ratio of the Hornet, and the exceptional low-speed handling characteristics, new manoeuvres were constantly being introduced into the display. Opposing solo Cliff Skelton was at this time perfecting a low-speed and heart-stopping 'tail walk' across the field . . .

I next saw the team in action a month later, when the Blue Angels gave a display at El Toro. The performance in front of the crowd was slick and precise. The Hornets looked lethal. It looked tremendously impressive. Unseen, but equally impressive from my point of view, was the insight into the many hours of practice that had preceded it.

30
Full Circle

Once again I was immersed in the demanding world of fighter design, and teaching aircraft design to a new generation of enthusiastic students. My weekends now gave the opportunity for flying a variety of smaller aircraft. All challenging in their own way . . .

I eased my stick a fraction to the right to level the wings as our two aircraft came out of the gentle left hand bank where we had been circling out over the channel between Los Angeles Harbour and the island of Catalina, just visible between banks of low stratus. Wings level, I scanned the sky through the bubble canopy of my French-built Robin, carefully checking for other traffic, then looked back at the aircraft riding off to my left. Propeller shining in the sun and resplendent in a red, white and blue sunburst, it was a mirror image of my own aircraft. Twenty feet off my left wingtip fellow pilot Rick Remelin was grinning across the intervening space.

A product of the eighties, the little Robin could give a creditable account of itself in aerobatics, but was stuffed full of sophisticated avionics which made it capable of transporting me through the intricacies of the Air Traffic Control System in comfort, yet still be a fun machine to fly.

As my logbooks slowly filled with a variety of aircraft, looking back I was struck with the thought that as I gained in experience the differences seemed smaller. The aircraft were, after all, just machines. It was fascinating to see how engineers and designers had solved different problems. But the aircraft themselves were just contrivances of metal, wood, fabric and plastic. Tools to do a specific job.

It's the pilots who make the difference. Pilots as a breed tend to be rather matter of fact. They fly for a profession and sometimes look askance at the notion that anyone would think their way of life out of the ordinary. But listen sometimes to test pilots, bush pilots or instructors as they let drop some nugget of experience. I'm still learning. I'm indebted to those military and civilian pilots with whom I've shared cockpits around the world.

In particular I thank former Naval test pilot Joel Premsalaar. Joel started his career flying floatplanes from the deck of a battleship, and rounded off his military career flying some rather hairy test hops in Navy jets. Now *there* is a story. Joel took the time to show me how to really *fly* a Bonanza. Some of the tricks are not in the book, but as aids to survival, they are good ones.

As one who now spends his working life designing aircraft that will be around for many years, it is instructive to see where the future might lead us.

What next? The aircraft designed by competing teams are now very similar in behaviour, with handling qualities determined by the computers of their fly-by-wire control systems, rather than the idiosyncrasies of aerodynamics which drove former generations of designers and flight test engineers wild with exasperation. Aircraft shapes are changing dramatically. Powerplants are more powerful and more reliable. The areas of the unknown are shrinking in aircraft design.

But pilot physiology is still very much the same and it is a fact that the pilots cannot take as much g-force as the aircraft. So the emphasis is changing in that field. Pilots must now master complex systems rather than the techniques of stick and rudder as in former days.

But the challenges are still there in different forms. Flying of itself is a series of challenges. First solo, gaining the various ratings and advancing to more complex machines are all rewarding. Flying a Piper Cub down to a cross-wind landing is just as challenging as scorching across the landscape at a significant fraction of the speed of sound.

I have had an enjoyable opportunity to sample a wide variety of flying machines. All unique in their own way, from jets to sailplanes.

Vintage airplanes and warbirds are again different, nostalgic and in their own way just as challenging to fly as more modern machines . . .

But that, as they say, is another story.

171

Index